VETERAN BEHIND!!!
FOREWORD BY KEN J. ROCHON, JR., PHD
DANIEL R. FAUST & ROBERT W. JONES

Stories From:
Demetrius Booth
Jeffrey Hall
Stefan Hobbs
Lisa Kraft
Gary Michiel Montiel
David Nordel
Kurt Porter
John Ready
Marilyn Richards
Yesenia Vazquez—Rosa
and more...

Revised & Updated

TRANSFORMATIONAL STORIES OF CURRENT AND FELLOW SERVICE MEMBERS TO HELP YOU ON YOUR NEXT MISSION IN LIFE

Leave No Veteran Behind!!!
by

Daniel R. Faust and Robert W. Jones

Foreword by Ken J. Rochon, Jr., PhD

With These Contributing Authors:

David Nordel, Marilyn Richards, Yesenia Vazquez-Rosa, John Ready, Demetrius Booth, Jeffrey Hall, Granny Lisa Kraft, Michiel Montiel, Stefan Hobbs, Jr., and Kurt Porter

Copyright © 2023 by Daniel R. Faust & Robert W. Jones

All rights reserved. This book or any portion thereof may not be reproduced or used in any manner whatsoever without the express written permission of Daniel R. Faust and Robert W. Jones (Learn & Live daniel.r.faust@gmail.com))

Printed in the United States of America
First Printing, 2023

ISBN for Print Editions (979-8-8689-7160-0)
ISBN for Electronic Editions (979-8-8689-7161-7)

Table of Contents

Mission

Vision

Foreword

    By Ken J. Rochon, Jr., PhD

1. **Clear the Beds** David Nordel

2. **Breaking the Fear** Marilyn Richards

3. **Saying "Yes" to You** Yesenia Vazquez-Rosa

4. **Internal Surgery** John Ready

5. **I See Men as Trees** Demetrius Booth

6. **Destiny Calling: Warrior of the West Side** Jeffrey Hall

7. **Superhero Life Lessons** Robert W Jones

8. **Sharing the Pain** Granny Lisa Kraft

9. **You are Worthy** Michiel "All Mike" Montiel

10. **The Great American Scream Machine** Daniel Faust

11. Family Ties
      Stefan Hobbs Jr

12. Oceans of Wisdom Kurt
    Porter

13. Contact the Authors

Mission

Two hundred thousand military members leave the service every year. Roughly 18 million plus Americans are veterans. This is only approximately 6% of the US population, so it is hard to find our brothers and sisters. From homelessness to mental health issues to financial difficulties, etc., we are all struggling or were in the struggle overall. We don't have to be in the fight alone.

Leave No Veteran Behind!!! is a book comprised of 12 veterans – past and present – sharing our struggles, for two reasons:

1. To show you that "you are not alone".

2. To demonstrate that you can break free from the trials, pain, mess, and wounds, to find your testimony, purpose, and message, and to grow in wisdom.

It has been just too long to see the struggling veteran and the despair of leaving the service, with no help in sight. We all have a mission and a team of brethren waiting for you to find it. There are amazing missions waiting to be created, and we want to help you see this for yourself.

This is more than a book; it is movement for the world to see that "Superheroes" do exist. They are **you**.

Ready to transform,
Daniel Faust

Vision

This book is not your normal book. Each chapter could be its own book. As you read each chapter, you see, hear, and feel each veteran's story. Some will read like a fiction book; other chapters will read like a life manual, while others will be summary of live-interview transcripts.

What are the threads that bind this book together/

1. We are all veterans who share snippets of our military.

2. We all share our unique but also common struggles while in the service and when we left.

3. We have looked at our lives and now share our life lessons – "Superhero Tactics" – so you can "Learn and Live" rather than "Live and Learn".

4. We have all found our mission now, and we love to serve you to get you to yours.

In summary, our vision for you is for you to "thrive" – not just "survive" – in your transformation journey. You have a bigger mission than just the military one that you proudly served. No matter if you served 30 days or 30 years, you are valued, called, redeemed, and an integral part of a bigger community.

You are a veteran; and we won't leave you or any of our brethren, behind.

Let the transformation begin!!!

Foreword

I've always been inspired by those who serve. When Daniel and Robert invited me to write a foreword for their book with leaders who understand what it is to make the ultimate sacrifice, I was honored to be included.

My Dad served in Vietnam, and I learned as a 5-year-old what it was like to have my dad away for a year, hoping he would come back alive and healthy. He never pressured me to serve, nor did he discourage me from following in his footsteps.

Although my service in the U.S. Army Transportation Corps (after being commissioned a 2nd Lieutenant out of Johns Hopkins University R.O.T.C. program) could never compare to my dad's assignments or anyone else's seeing combat, I feel it is important that every person serve their country for two years both for the experience and for doing their part.

Regardless of any of my entrepreneurial endeavours, whether it be my disc jockey company, my photography company, or now my publishing company, I have always given back to those who serve in our military. Whether it be discounted or free services, it is my little way of showing respect and staying connected to our heroes.

I've travelled to over one hundred countries, and when I return home to America, I smile and feel like the luckiest man alive. The military tours remind us how great our land is and why we must defend it.

No matter how many movies (such as **Blackhawk Down**,

Hacksaw Ridge, *The Outpost*, *Saving Private Ryan*, etc.) one watches about battles and war, it is not possible ever to understand the adrenaline; the not knowing if this is your last day, last minute to live, and the toll that anxiety and loss may have on the mind and spirit. These only come from being there.

My recommendation is to embrace every person in uniform with a handshake and a look in their eyes to share they made a difference. Because war is not fair. And it isn't glamorous when things aren't going right, and support is not available.

Just as these veterans will inspire you with their transformational stories, I encourage you to share them with other Americans who have served and with others who would benefit from these words of wisdom.

The best way you can thank these heroes is to provide a review, a post on social media, and to let them know they made a difference. It is our duty to honor their service by helping their work serve as a legacy piece.

A book is only as powerful as the impact it can make. So, share its glory and take a photo representing you holding up and standing for those who protect and serve our country.

My ten-year-old son Kenny is a Boy Scout, and he is aware of how many Boy Scouts go on to our great academies to become better leaders. Much like a parent has a fiercely protective attitude when it comes to their children being safe, so too, does the soldier for his fellow brothers and sisters in arms.

Kenny values life and is in awe of anyone that would die for our country. I remind him that heroes don't desire to die; that's what makes them heroes. One of my bigger lessons is sharing that believing in, being courageous and standing up for your country allows us to live with less fear and more freedom.

There are some organizations I have served and supported because of who they are for veterans.

They will all get a copy of this book to share with those on a mission to celebrate our heroes.

Stand for the flag at noon and enjoy the best BBQ in the world - https://mission-bbq.com.

Most amazing events for veterans transitioning back to civilian and corporate opportunities - https://americandreamu.org

Consider visiting this site - https://amillionthanks.org/letter/

Over 12 million letters have been sent to veterans abroad sharing the writer's appreciation for all they do. Send your letter and it could save a life or, at the very least, make someone Smile.

Ken J. Rochon, Jr., PhD

Clear the Beds

By David Nordel

Within the shadows of trauma, two steadfast companions loom: post-traumatic stress disorder (PTSD) and moral injury. As the owner of both, I have forged an intimate relationship with these silent warriors that accompany me daily. They simultaneously remind me how easy it is to quit and how rewarding it is to follow my intention and determination to not quit.

Moral injury embodies the psychological and spiritual anguish that ensues when one witnesses or engages in actions that transgress their deeply ingrained moral beliefs and values. While often associated with high-stress professions like the military, healthcare, and first responders, moral injury can manifest in any context where individuals confront morally challenging situations.

The weight of moral injury has shaped my existence in profound ways. As a military veteran, I found myself caught in a web of moral dilemmas, forced to make excruciating decisions that violated my core principles. The toll this took on my soul was immeasurable, plunging me into a sea of guilt and shame and a sense of betrayal. In accepting these experiences, I have sought to harness their transformative energy, using my stories and emotions as a catalyst for helping to heal others and enlightening those in helping roles who may not have experienced similar traumas.

The world has a dire need for understanding. When I received three phone calls in a single day from friends and family scattered across the nation, all seeking clarity on moral injury, it ignited the realization that many others are also grappling with this concept. Moral injury, distinct from PTSD, delves into the inner conflict that arises from violating one's moral compass. It elicits emotions such as guilt, shame, and a shattered trust in oneself and others. Unlike PTSD, it does not stem solely from combat or traumatic experiences but can emerge from a variety of contexts.

The prevalence of PTSD and moral injury among veterans in the United States is alarmingly high. Both conditions need multifaceted support and assistance to create healing. Veterans' stories, often left untold, hold the key to unlocking empathy and understanding.

Beyond a fleeting "Thank you for your service" lies a world of untold narratives. Engaging veterans in conversation and inviting them to share their stories, unlocks profound connections and bridges understanding. We all face complexities and challenges, and we all can set an intention and determination not to quit. Together, let us march onward, offering support, compassion, and a listening ear to those whose journeys have been shaped by PTSD and moral injury. Onward!

This is my journey:

At times, we experience events that seem unreal when we reflect on them, almost as if they never happened. Before I started to write the first word of this chapter, I called a dear friend and one of my leaders during a unique and trying time. I will call him Doc. He was also the leader who carried a tremendous burden as we made decisions of incredible magnitude. With his permission and collaboration, this chapter will be ours to share from a joint perspective.

Doc and I worked through clearing the beds and preparing for what would be a major operation during the surge in Iraq.

Clearing the beds means to empty an entire hospital ahead of a major military offensive. It is prepping for mass casualties. Those of us who are critical of our leaders and think we could do it better, can more deeply appreciate those who take on such decisions and responsibilities. We can better realize how lonely it can be for the one who must make the call and then execute it.

When I was growing up in a rural community, I was exposed to leaders in less traditional ways. My examples of leaders included farmers (of course), business owners, a baseball coach or two, cops, firefighters, and all the elected officials around. As I watched the farmers conduct their business and daily operations, they made decisions constantly: *Do I send the cow to slaughter? Do I plant or not plant? Do I sell or buy?* They also decide what they can and can't do; vacations are but a dream, and supporting their kids and their growth drives priorities. It amazed me how natural it seemed. These men and women would just start by putting the decision into motion and then managing and leading it. Sometimes it didn't go well, but mostly it seemed *easy.* It wasn't until I started to lead people and manage resources with high value that I understood what goes on in the leader's mind—the lost sleep, the seeking counsel and advice, and the reading and research that go with preparation. It takes constant work to be the most informed and capable leader you can be before you make big decisions, and all the while, you manage the dynamics that go along with change.

When my grandfather decided to move his entire farming operation from the California northern coast to the northern valley, I am sure he had many conversations and sleepless nights. There were kids to consider (my mother would move in the middle of her high school years); and he had to ask advice from my grandmother. In the end, when it came time to decide, it was his decision, and all that comes with it weighed on him.

When asked how he felt about making the decision to invade Normandy in June of 1944, General Eisenhower said that the best night's sleep he got was after he made the decision to go, for at that moment, it was up to others to execute the mission. I am sure he worried, and he definitely led and managed through the end of the war and beyond. But in this case, his weight of command was immense in that he had lots of advice, data, and history to work with. It is a lonely existence when you consider all that, and the whole world is looking at you to make the call, set the direction, and move out. Once you start things like that in motion, there is no going back. When we were told to clear the beds in 2008, it was not done in haste, and it was not done without heartfelt and deep thought.

In the spring of 2008, we had many operations going on during the surge that brought unique influxes to our trauma center. At times, we experienced deeply tragic moments. One dynamic that had started to rise was that the enemy was continually harassing part of Baghdad with rockets and mortars. This attack would require significant operations to neutralize and ultimately eliminate the threat. This was one of those decisions that I alluded to earlier, and I am sure it was not taken lightly, as it meant that we would have significant casualties to achieve the mission. This event started the domino effect that would come into our medical world and into our military responsibilities to execute our portion of the mission. This would soon become a deeply dividing emotional event between leaders of a medical unit filled with people who were torn between the responsibilities that come with both. In this case, the core values that drive each of these professions would collide and drive human emotions in a way I had never experienced before or since.

To set the stage for those who are not steeped in military doctrine and operations, there is a whole process to how you fight and go to war. It is not as simple as taking some tanks over there and taking that ground or getting the enemy—it is very complex and requires extreme logistics, planning, resource massing, and just-in-time training. Each operation is unique and requires collaboration between the services involved. All of this must be ready to go before the "tanks" are sent forward. In these situations, the medical piece is also complex. For example, recent intelligence reports that before the Russians invaded Ukraine, a key indicator of the imminent invasion was the fact that the medical units had started to bring blood supplies to the frontlines. This is one of those building blocks that must be in place before you send in the tanks. In our case, as we prepared to eliminate this threat, we knew there would be multiple casualties over a course of many days. So, we received the order to "Clear the beds!"

"Clear the beds" sounds like a hard and painful event and a lot of work. In reality, in most non-combat hospitals, this is easier than it sounds. The challenge is regarding the critical care beds for extremely ill people. Our situation was odd and complex. There are often emotions attached to any patient we care for, especially with the amount of skill and expertise required to keep these people alive, as we try to send them home to their loved ones. There were three categories of patients in the hospital at the time: Allies (Americans or other allies, including civilian personnel), Iraqis (those who are indigenous to the country— men, women, and children—and non-combatants), and the enemy (yes, we took care of the enemy right alongside the rest).

In our hospital, the American wounded were evacuated in twenty-four to forty-eight hours, no matter how badly hurt they were. This was an amazing feat performed daily by incredible people; we got the patients home to more definitive care that was closer to their loved ones. If patients were allied members, it was fast but maybe not as fast; still, we got you home, too. For the indigenous patients who were severely injured and required intensive care, our hospital was almost always the best place to be. Here they had the best chance of survival and rehabilitation. So often, we had many intensive care beds full of indigenous patients — yes, including the enemy. These patients (these people, rather) became part of our lives, as did the assigned Soldiers, Sailors, Airmen, and Marines who guarded the enemy patients 24/7. It was common to look down the bay of patients and see three or four guards sitting at the bedside. We did it all.

The healthcare in Iraq at this time was fractured, and most civilian facilities didn't have the capabilities we had. It always amounted to dropping them down a level or two in care when we moved them. The goal was to get them as healthy as possible before we moved them, and they mainly went to the hospitals in Baghdad. This happened frequently —usually one or two at a time—and our docs took them on the helicopters to Baghdad.

We had dedicated and highly passionate professional people who were charged with these transfers. We were all passionate about our patients, no matter who they were. I watched, on more than one occasion, as an enemy patient would throw urine or feces at our Airmen. I helped clean up a few times after these events, and yet after all that, our caregivers continued to care for each of them like they were the most important persons in the room. I bet you have a bit of emotion and many questions right now. Multiply them by hundreds, and you can get to the place where I am going to take you.

The beds were cleared for a few reasons. One was because an allied member needed a bed, so room was made, usually through transfer. We also cleared the beds in the case of a mass casualty event; and we cleared the beds when military planning and doctrine dictated that the beds would be empty prior to a major operation where many casualties were expected. Once this order was placed, it was on the hospital command staff to execute it. The person who held the full responsibility was the commander — the leader of the whole smash. Remember, this book is about *quitting* or *not quitting*, so I will tell you now that the actions of the leader and the navigation he had to make in what I am about to describe were no less than amazing. I don't know more than a handful of commanders in my time who would have maintained their temper, grace, and respect any better.

So, yes, we had civilians in our hospital and intensive units; some had been there for months and had undergone multiple surgeries. We knew their names, and some even had family members come to visit. They were there so long an odd dynamic in the middle of a war, right? Yes, we also had the enemy. No visitors, but surely there for a long while and well known to us. And we always had our own, getting ready to be moved to Germany and then home. We were usually full. When the order came to clear the beds, we had enough going on in the hospital that we needed to make difficult decisions quickly and execute them with precision and expertise.

We had the right people for all of this, but what we hadn't anticipated was the added dimension of knowing what may come of the patients we had to "clear." We knew the practices of the Iraqi medical systems; they were not like our own. In this case, they did not have the resources to sustain these patients. There was a high probability that after all these months of care, these people would not survive. In the eyes of some of our team, they were convinced that this was true, and, worse yet, they felt that if they participated in the clearing of the beds, then they were essentially "killing them." Things were said like, "I will not participate in euthanasia." The emotions ran hot, and quickly there became two camps.

Remember, I told you, this needed to be planned and executed quickly; there wasn't time to vote or develop elaborate alternatives. We were going to do the normal transfer process, just in mass and volume, and quickly. All hands on deck, as it were. Well, we had a problem. Many of the key people in that process felt that the oath they took was of the highest calling in this situation. Higher than their officer-ship, their command position, or the direct military orders given to them. They did not want to participate, and they were highly emotional about it—they were in the decision stages of "do I or don't I *quit.*"

This was a powerful moment, under direct orders, while in a combat zone, and the ramifications of disobeying could be up to execution (no, we don't do that anymore, but it is still on the books). You can face extreme discipline and stand to lose an awful lot in the end. Here we were in a swirl of emotions around patients we knew, a process that was not desirable—morals, values, credos, and medical professional beliefs. All of it was colliding.

This is when you are defined as a leader; these are the moments when you are all alone (see a similar story in **Make the Tough Call** in my first book).

My deepest personal memory of this as the Chief was interacting with my fellow Airmen and medical professionals who were absolutely against it. I had my orders; the boss was clear, and now we needed to move out and clear the beds. We knew the potential outcomes, and we knew who might be filling that bed in the next twenty-four to forty-eight hours: our men and women who were headed to the fight. As I spoke to the staff—some new to the Air Force and others who had been around for a long time—and listened to their concerns, I had mixed emotions. I am a Registered Nurse, and I had a calling and an oath. But I am also an American Airman, and I had my orders. It was a double dilemma, for sure. I felt these individuals' passion and their desire to honor both the oath and the order and make it all better. The fact was, we had to pick the best of a few bad choices and then commit to it and execute or *quit.* This is where leaders show their true colors, and how they shape the decision and execute it matters forever.

I would like to say that everyone came around to the belief that clearing the beds was okay because our fighters were going in them and because our orders were our orders and disobeying was treasonous. I wish that were the case. We had congressional inquiries that lasted long after we all rotated back to the world, and we had anger. Frankly, we lost a few people in the areas of enthusiasm or commitment. Those losses were few, though, because the leader did his magic. He listened, he heard, he explained why (both his reasons and the mission), he gave clear expectations and desired outcomes, he ensured we had what we needed to make it happen, he had our backs and our fronts when the exterior forces played into all this, and most of all, he *cared* about all of us. No matter what side of the issue we fell on, he respected our beliefs and wanted us all to have some foundation after it was over to stay, not *quit*, and to be ready for the next mission. There is always a next mission, a next tough decision, and a next order that sounds like "clear the beds" that we will need to be ready for.

Did we clear the beds? Yes, with military precision. Did we like the results that occurred for our indigenous patients? Of course not. All of us wished we had a better bad option. Did we quit? Maybe some quit on the Air Force that day; maybe some dumped the good attitude and commitment. But I didn't see anybody *quit,* because the real reason to do that is more about how the leader handles it than it is about the actual issue at hand. We cleared the beds, we did it well, and we met the mission. The difficult part of all of this, however, was that the major operation that drove this directive was cancelled. We never received a mass casualty, and we never got any of our patients back. There was no way to predict that situation and no way we could have taken the risk. The leadership challenge that goes with this part of the story requires a daily commitment to the ideals I mentioned—we were led in a way that didn't produce *quitters.* It created future leaders, showed us an example to follow as we continued on, and definitely showed us how to make tough calls.

Superhero Tactic 1: Embrace Supportive Healing: Recognize that selfcare alone may not be enough to heal the deep wounds of your journey. Seek help and support from others, putting your ego aside to allow for genuine healing and growth.

Superhero Tactic 2: Harness Resilient Energy: Acknowledge the authentic and powerful energy stemming from injury and trauma. Channel this energy towards positive transformation and personal growth. Learn to shift its polarity into a force that empowers and strengthens you.

Superhero Tactic 3: Master Your Attitude: Your attitude shapes your reality. Embrace a positive outlook regardless of what challenges life hrows your way. Utilize the energy of positivity to manage obstacles and conquer adversities with determination and grace.

Lessons from "Clear the Beds"

- Respect toward those who disagree with your direction sometimes grows new followers.
- Listening to all viewpoints can steady the emotions and calm the seas.
- Setting the direction and providing clarity are life skills in every avenue we operate in — your team and, better yet, your family will love you for it.
- If it is your call to make, gather data and then make the call. If you hesitate, you may lose your teammates and your command.
- The best decision is sometimes the best of a few really bad options—be okay with that and know that it is not going to magically change.
- Teams succeed and fail on the back of the leader — build a tough team before a crisis.
- Have your people's backs and fronts—they need to be able to focus. This includes your kids and spouse or significant other.

Breaking the Fear

By Marilyn Richards

I sat down with Daniel Faust, Founder of **Leave No Veteran Behind,** to share my story in an interview style. This chapter will read a bit differently, as it will be a Q&A session. I hope whatever you might be struggling with that you find hope in my story.

Daniel: Hey, Marilyn, thanks for joining,

Marilyn: No, thank you! I appreciate it.

Daniel: You're welcome. So, this is all about you, and this is all about how you moved from broken to healed, so you have to go back into the past a little bit. So, our first question for you is -
Who is Marilyn as a child and teen?

Marilyn: My childhood was not without a lot of heartache. As a child, I was always this active, bright, bubbly sweet girl. Classmates would write in my yearbook at the end of the year things like, "Stay sweet and smile always." Those kinds of things made a huge impression on me so I would take those comments to heart.

When I was in elementary school, the Yard Duty Supervisor would call me "Sunshine" and the Crossing Guard Lady would call me "Smiley." Despite what was going on in my family, I always acted like everything was okay and always wanted to promote positivity as an overall optimistic child, no matter what bad thing was going on around me.

As a teen, I was struggling with my parents' divorce and the way they separated. My mom made me go to church. It was there that I found an outlet through the Youth Group, and it helped me to channel much of the insecurities and adolescent struggles that we often faced— like peer pressure, hormones, acne, and family problems. I was 12 or 13 when I got saved and accepted Jesus Christ as my Lord and Savior.

There was something very warm and welcoming regarding Christianity that drew me in like a warm, secure blanket.

It was the Youth Group that became my "go-to", along with journaling and writing poetry to help process and internalize my feelings, as I was never an outspoken child. Unless I got mad, of course. Then I'd have outbursts if I was mad. But any other time, I would listen to my parents or any older person and respect that they were the adult, and I didn't have a say, so you just accept what you're told and do as you're told.

Growing up in the '80s before technology and social media—life was very different back then. I often played outside and went to friends' houses to hang out. We would spend time together at the mall, go to the park and get together at family BBQ's and special occasions. I grew up in the era that you do not to talk back to your parents or any adults and you are respectful, or you'd get a whooping.

I think I was like 6 or 7 when the traumatic event unfolded between my parents. When my dad found out that my Mom was cheating on him, it turned out to be a huge scene. The picture is in pieces in my head, but when talking to my cousin Harry, he explained the whole scenario because he was there. He ended up coming over to rescue us. He said the cops surrounded the house because my dad was so livid about the affair, he pulled a rifle on my Mom, and she begged him not to shoot her.

I remember when my sisters and I were in the doorway of her bedroom crying and screaming for our dad to stop and not hurt our mom. That image burned into my memory, and I still carry it this day. My cousin Harry told me the whole story, but it was all because my mom—who came from the Philippines—left my dad for her boyfriend at the time, who later became my stepdad because he could give her a better and more secure life.

My stepdad had retired as a Lt. Col. in the Air Force Reserves. He used to be a pilot for American Airlines and would often fly in /out of San Francisco. My dad had retired as a Tech Sergeant in the Air Force, and he had to work his way up to a foreman when he started out at Budweiser. Both of my parents never finished school. My dad got his GED when he was in the military and my mom would work different odd jobs over the years, but—like most Asians—ultimately depend on their significant other to support them.

I did not want to be stuck between parents and I didn't want a stepmom or stepdad, but it was something I unfortunately had to accept, which made joining the military and "embracing the suck" more acceptable.

I just remember thinking how much I couldn't wait to graduate high school so I could get away from all the drama, toxicity, brokenness, and family bickering. I couldn't wait to get out on my own and live my life away from my family. That's what I did. I joined the military.

After this trauma, what lies did you believe?

Some of the lies that I believed for a long time was my mom being at fault or was to blame for splitting the family up. I believed in the lies that it was not okay to talk about problems outside of the family.

Later, when I was unfortunately sexually assaulted in the Navy, I believed for the longest time that it was my fault.

When you were an adult, you joined the Navy and Air Force. What was that like for you?

I was 18 when I joined, excited about leaving home and my hometown. I didn't feel like I had a home or family to go to because it was broken. I decided that when I turned 18, I would join the Navy, along with my twin sister, and take advantage of all that the military had to offer. I was young and naïve, so it was easy for me to get suckered into going in undesignated.

As a result, I ended up going into one of the worst divisions in the Air Department, known as the V-2 Division—launch and recovery. They had the worst reputation for being the most undermanned, under-qualified, negative, low-morale and toxic environment. In my young mind, I was like, "I can do this. I'm not going to let the Navy break my free spirit and bubbliness." Little did I know how much it would cost me.

I was stationed on the USS Carl Vinson, a nuclear Nimitz-class carrier. The first two years were the most awesome and amazing experience of my life. I had fun!

Once I struck the rate (in other terms, MOS) of Aviation Boatswain's Mate, that's when everything went downhill. I moved into what was called the Waist Work Center. The Waist is located underneath the landing area of the flight deck where catapults 3 and 4 are—the slingshot that shoots naval aircraft off the flight deck. If you have ever seen **Behind Enemy Lines** with Joaquin de Almeida and Owen Wilson, (the film was based on our ship), you'll notice the catapults when they get ready to launch but then the aircraft gets grounded, so they never do fly off. That was my job. Once I got qualified, I was constantly overworked.

I used to work about 22 hours every day we were out to sea conducting flight operations. I would launch from the Waist, hurry up and run to the bow of the ship to launch from cats 1 and 2, and then run back to the Waist and prep for landing. On top of poor morale, toxic leadership, and long hours, it was a recipe for disaster.

Unfortunately, I experienced sexual assault at the hands of someone I knew, and it ruined the rest of my enlisted term. I just wanted to get out. I sucked-it-up, finished my time and got out.

I was on terminal leave when the events of September 11, 2001, occurred. That was when I made the decision to cross over into the AF and it was such a great transition. Unfortunately, I had a hard time adjusting because I was a Sailor first, Airmen second. I did not feel like I belonged. I felt very disoriented. It was very hard for me to adjust to a different way of life and culture.

The Air Force, however, has the best quality of life out of all the branches, and it was such an amazing time, despite feeling like a fish out of water. I didn't stay in for very long. I ended up getting out during a Force-Shaping phase when the AF was minimizing its workforce by filling in critical career fields, minimizing overmanned career fields, and getting rid of different jobs. I got out one year earlier than expected.

After your MST (Military Sexual Trauma), which is stacked with childhood, who did you become?

Since my mind blocked out the incident, I went into "work" mode. I just remember thinking and feeling like I can't wait to get out. I just wanted to finish my time and get out. Suck-it-up and move on.

There was a drive within me to just get away from everything— from childhood to my time in the Navy.

The Navy made me a hard worker. Being in the Navy and having a hard work ethic, I became a workaholic.

I moved away from home and have lived far away ever since. Even when I crossed over into the Air Force, I was always trying to find something to do. After I got out, I thrust myself into full-time work, full-time school and full-time ministry while trying to do a side hustle in business selling life insurance. I had this need to stay busy all the time.

I have always had a heart to serve others and being involved in church and doing things that would be beneficial for community service was my "go-to." It was this "go, go, go" and "do, do, do" mentality.

So, you became this very independent workaholic kind of person. Now, did that stay after the MST? So that tells me where that what happened with the childhood till the Navy, what about the MST? Did that amplify who you became, or did it change you even more?

It amplified because I've always been like a silent sufferer type. I've never been really outspoken. There are times when I was a kid that I would have little temper tantrums, but for the most part, I'd keep to myself.

I never said anything. I just wanted to get away. I would never talk about what happened. I'd kind of sweep it under the carpet and pretend like it wasn't there. That's how I kind of took the incident. I pretended like nothing happened. I sucked it up. That suck it up mentality is very hard core, but that's the way it was back then.

As I understand it, if our listeners and readers are understanding, this was 1998. A little history with the Air Force and Navy—the Sexual Assault Response program that you are all indoctrinated right now. Almost a 20-year program now, but back then it was not a commonality to have those safety nets and community to go and to build that.

So, you quickly left the Navy, and you went into the Air Force. Do you think that ST in the childhood made it even harder to make that transition into the Air Force?

No, it was not being able to adjust and adapt into a different culture and environment that really affected me. I blocked it out of my mind as soon as I left the Navy. I left everything that I associated with the Navy behind when I left.

It wasn't until my best friend encouraged me to file for my disability in 2012, where she brought back things that I forgot. For example, she reminded me that I called her the next day to tell her what happened. Slowly, I started dealing with the details of the incident, putting the bits and pieces together, but not without her help. Finally, things started flooding back to me, but this was in 2012, so we're talking about twelve years later.

So, as we're making this transition where you became, as you said, a 'workaholic,' you went over and just stayed aggressive in what you were doing—the "yes" person: full-time ministry, full-time work, fulltime college and everything else.

What was the breaking point? To seek the truth? Because especially if you blocked it out, you don't have to seek the truth because you don't know it existed.

Well, it started in 2012 when my best friend, Judy told me that I needed to get help. I took what she said to heart, and it hit me that I really needed help in dealing with trauma of sexual assault in the Navy. I'd been running around, sucking up, pretending like things are okay for twelve years, when I really hadn't dealt with it since I left the Navy. That was, until I decided to file for my VA disability in November 2012.

It sparked me on a journey towards healing by seeking out different ways and different therapeutic methods to help me process the negative thoughts and feelings that trauma had led me to believe. I was starting to see the pain clearly and recognize the symptoms of PTSD that I was masking through denial, a "suck-it-up" mentality, and the need to stay busy all the time. One day in 2018, it just hit me, how unhappy, empty, and discouraged I felt. I felt stuck. Like a gerbil or hamster spinning around on a wheel that's never ending. My life wasn't going anywhere.

There was this dog park behind my apartment where I lived in Lancaster that I would often take my dog to and let her run around. I would often sit there and talk to God. Many times, I would be praying for help and for a way out. I recognized that I needed a change and that I needed to leave where I was living at the time.

I was in a dead-end job where upper leadership kept me from moving forward. They were never going to tell me that I would never receive my clearance. I had to find out on my last day out-processing that someone up the chain was keeping me from getting my clearance. It was a devastating blow to my already fragile state but receiving that piece of knowledge helped me to know I made the right decision to leave the Air Force as a civilian and move on to better adventures.

Except for the Covid pandemic. That was nuts. I started waitressing just to keep my sanity and get out of the house!

How did the process start? What were the steps to start that process? Was it through chaplains? Was it through mental health? What type of resources helped you start this process?

I had already started the process in 2012 when I filed for my disability. However, when I made the decision to do something about this stuck point, that's when things started changing for the good for me. Prioritizing my mental health and self-care became my focus, which eventually led me to where I am now—stable, happy, and at peace.

I started throwing my applications out there. I started applying to jobs in Missouri and Florida. Even my hometown of Vallejo, California, just to see where I could go. The job that I have now opened up the opportunity for me to start my life over and prioritize my mental health and self-care. It opened me up to a whole new area where I did not know anyone; a whole new job, a whole new industry. I left everything behind that I knew to start my life over.

That's huge because Marilyn and I have a history, even before this book started. I met her when she was in California through a Facebook Group called Vetprener Tribe, and everything else, and you were wrestling about making that decision.

You wanted to write a memoir about your dad, and I think that's when all that stuff, and if I remember correctly, you were at a high level in the government at the time, and you decided to make a pivot, so you took mental health that seriously. It was a job change and a job decrease, just so you could take care of yourself mentally, emotionally, spiritually.

Yes, I was a GS-5 in the government pay scale system. I was a secretary at the base and worked for one of the biggest branches at the research lab, but then I took a GS-4 part-time position, because I didn't want to completely be without a job. I knew I needed at least a part time job while I got myself together. At first, I hesitated and wondered if I should, but I just decided to take a jump and just do it. It has been the best thing that I've ever done for MYSELF.

And that's good to hear. So, our next question is, and for everybody, because again, from what you said, if I remember correctly, the incident happened in the Navy in the late nineties, early 2000s. Now, it's 2023. Why is it important to heal?

There's something I said earlier. um, When I hit that breaking point in 2018 and thought to myself that there's got to be more to life than this. As a Christian, my faith is very, very important to me and Jesus is very, very important to me. One of the Scriptures that I've held very dear to my life for many years is Jeremiah 29:11 when the Lord says, "My plans are plans of good and not evil. Plans to give you hope and a future and an expected outcome." I could never see that before.

I always held onto that Scripture, but I didn't really understand what that Scripture meant, because I've always been clouded in this, in this darkness, always in survival mode—just wanting to get through today. I can't think about tomorrow. I can only think about getting through today.

It's so important for me to want to experience what Jesus came to this earth to do, which is to give us life, and that much more abundantly (John 10:10). I've always wanted the abundant life, but I didn't know how to get it.

I know my salvation is secure in Him. I know that the message of the Cross is so powerful, and the blood of Jesus is so powerful. I've always been strong spiritually, but it was in the rest of the areas of my life where I was a mess.

Emotionally and mentally, such a mess, and you know, when you're struggling with post-traumatic stress… when you're struggling with anxiety, you're deep in depression, it's so hard to get out of it. You get stuck. It's like a hamster going round and round.

Just another Groundhog Day, you're just trying to survive, and it's just no way to live. There's this inner warrior in me that wants to get out of this survival mode. I want to thrive. There's a person in you who wants something more out of life. Sure, you put things on your calendar, and you plan for things, but at the same time it's like a daily fight.

When you're struggling with PTSD, it's a daily fight to move forward.

We were made for a purpose. We were made to live life and give God glory. We have a purpose on this earth, and we need to fulfill that purpose, whatever it is. That's why it's important to heal so you can do what you've been called to do on this earth, whatever it is.

I wanted to heal so that way I can experience the beauty of life. What Jesus came to give in John 10:10, "I came that you might have life and have it more abundantly."

Why was it important to heal?

It was important for me to heal because I thought, "There's got to be more to life than this." Jeremiah 29:11 is one of my favorite Scriptures. I held on to that Scripture for many years, not being able to see it because PTSD, anxiety, and depression sort of envelops you into this darkness where your mind is always clouded and you're just trying to survive the day. I was in survival mode. In that sort of mentality, it's hard to really imagine a future, when you're just trying to make it through today. You plan and hope for things and put stuff on your calendar, but like the training that I had in the military—mission first, everything else later. You can only be strong for so long, until you get to a breaking point. For me, at this lowest point of my life, there had to be a change or breakthrough before the darkness tried to swallow me up.

God desires that we are full of peace, light, love, and joy. These are the things that come with salvation in Christ and so much more, but when you're dealing with trauma—the brain goes into this psychological state where your brain is searching for safety and peace. Due to the broken bond of trust, there is this need to put up walls and keep people at arm's length, because someone violated your boundary or someone or something disrupted your life to the point that you no longer feel safe, and there is no place to go that feels like home. You run and run until you can't run anymore. This survival mode mentality is exhausting. What was meant to be a temporary reaction that the body does in danger, slowly becomes a handicap, so you're walking around wounded but trying to keep it from bleeding with bandages. You got to cut deep into that wound and clean it out before it festers.

Healing is important because living this way—it's not a life. It's no way to live feeling broken, busted, and disgusted. It's no way to live feeling depressed, down, hopeless and tired all the time.

I think that's pretty awesome. Now it's 2023. After this book gets published and everything else, who and where is Marilyn now, physically, mentally, emotionally, and spiritually? Where you were 1020 years ago?

So much better today than where I was even like four years ago. I have a history of being iron-deficient and it was always a battle to have energy to do anything, but I'm a fighter. I'm a warrior. I'm constantly pushing myself. The military training that we get, it helps us to strive and to be more excellent.

One of the Air Force core values that I LOVE is excellence in everything that we do. You know, I'm always striving for that. Even in ministry, we're taught to be more excellent than our neighbor.

I would constantly push myself, but it's hard to do when you're always constantly challenged with health and mental health challenges. I feel happy. I feel free. I'm stable after all, like all these years, being unstable. It's a great feeling to be stable. Becoming a homeowner has been one of the most important milestones in my life that helped me to obtain peace and stability along with Christ's promise that peace is with us.

It's important to have a place that you can call home, a place that is a safety net for you. At the end of the day, you can come home and you don't have to worry about suffering acts of violence or strife or division or toxicity, because you created this haven for yourself. For me, to come home at the end of the day in peace, it's priceless.

I've made peace with my past, and now I'm ready to move forward. I'm ready to see Jeremy 29:11 fulfilled in my life.

Who and where is Marilyn now physically, mentally, emotionally, and spiritually?

Today, I feel happy and free. Physically, I am okay. I spent many years struggling with iron-deficiency anemia, so it was a constant fight to stay energized, because I was always anemic. Today, I am happy to say that I'm no longer iron-deficient. I found a doctor, when I moved to my new place, who took care of me and got it under control. Mentally, I feel stable. It took a combination of different therapies, therapeutic methods, grounding techniques, faith-based devotion, services, and prayer, writing/journaling, PTSD treatment centers and programs such as Warrior PATHH [Editor's Note: "Progressive and Alternative Training for

Helping Heroes"], helped break some of those negative patterns, self-inflicting thoughts, and lies that you believe about yourself. Putting myself first and focusing on self-care, learning to be kind to myself and not be so hard on myself are the little things that really help you to move forward. Emotionally, I'm stable now.

When I found that I was able to qualify for a house and utilize the VA home loan for the first time, it changed everything for me. All my life living in California, I never dreamed that I could be a homeowner. I was finally able get stable for once in my life. Having stability, a job that I love and enjoy, and my own space were tremendous to my recovery and ability to see the promise of a future. My future looks so bright. Whereas before, it was as if you're looking at the end of the tunnel. You're so far from it, but you keep striving towards it even though it's so far away. You hold on hoping to get to that light at the end of the tunnel, but the roadblocks that get in the way often become discouraging and make you want to give up. So, it's a daily fight. A daily fight to hope, to dream, to live.

Spiritually, I have always been strong. It wasn't until after my tour in the Navy when I rededicated my life to Christ and had this hunger to learn more about Jesus and grow in my faith. I spent 17 years actively involved in ministry. Every time the church doors were open, I was there. I love Jesus. He has kept me through some of the darkest times in my life. Recently, I've been watching The Chosen series on TV, and I just fell in love with Jesus all over again!! If it wasn't for my Savior, I would not be where I am now. It is through His love, His grace and the AMAZING LOVE and SUPPORT of family and friends that I am here.

What tactics have you gleaned that other veterans can learn from and live out?

I had a severe trigger in January 2020, and I almost fell into that deep, dark, black hole most suicidal victims get suckered into. The fear that I was going to do something stupid made me call out for help. I hardly ever use social media to tell my personal business or use it to share the things that I struggle deeply with. I've always been a silent sufferer type. But that day when I cried out on Facebook, it forever impacted my life. In my isolation and loneliness, I was too blind to see that people cared. Family and friends started pouring out their support and I had no idea that it would impact my life the way it did. I had no idea that people cared so much. It became a lifeline for me. It brought me through a hard year, especially when COVID happened, and we had to stay at home. Staying at home by mandatory orders was making my mental health even worse.

At the time, I was living in an apartment and sharing with 3 other roommates. I was hardly living there for 2 years when I was going on a third roommate. It felt too much like my old life in the military because people were always coming and going. Very unstable. On top of that, COVID and stay-at-home orders, while also dealing with PTSD. It was definitely a very challenging period.

First thing that I learned was that it is OKAY to ask for help. We don't have to feel isolated and alone. So many people are struggling out here, too. I'm used to suffering alone and not wanting to bother people with my problems, or "sucking it up" as I learned in the military. Compartmentalizing our emotions is great for combat, training, and hostile situations, but it's not applicable for everyday life in the civilian world. When I learned that it's okay to not be okay and find the courage to get help, some of those things I was carrying, I was able to lay down. Finally. Second, it's not just about talk therapy. Honestly, it's finding things that help you process your pain, whether it be art, music, gardening, baking, attending support groups, connecting with your community, and getting involved, or whatever it is! There are programs for everyone if you just look for them. Google has become my best friend! This goes along with also opening up about your pain.

You can't expect to heal if you don't want to open up and deal with it. There are a lot of veterans who walk around with festered wounds for 20-30-50 years. My dad is a Vietnam vet and did two combat tours. He has never shied away from sharing his story, but there are a lot of veterans who don't like to talk about their experiences. I used to be one of them. Let's sweep it in the closet and forget about it. That's fine and dandy, until you have to open the closet one day and those skeletons are staring back at you. Then what? Push it back in and close the door like we've been taught? How's that working out for you?

It wasn't until I made the decision in 2012—when I filed for my disability—to finally admit that I needed help. That's when I started seeking therapy, but that was just the beginning!

Someone once told me, "The more you talk about it, the more you heal." You first must start with yourself and be honest with yourself. You've got to be kind enough to yourself and love yourself enough to say, "No more suffering. Let's deal with it." Once I started talking about it, the more open I became, the lighter I've become.

Along with therapy, learning to incorporate wellness practices and therapeutic methods will help you stay grounded and be able to function. One of the biggest impacts on my journey to healing was doing wellness retreats and activities that help you deal with PTSD. One of those programs is called Warrior PATHH. There are 7 locations across the country. You are on-site for 7-days to learn and then take the rest of the program home to implement for 90-days into what ultimately turns into a lifestyle. It is one of the best programs out there for those who really struggle with PTSD.

Ultimately, the biggest thing I can recommend is giving Jesus a try. There is a lot of religious stigma, controversies, and heresies in the world regarding religion, religious ideals, and misconceptions, because of what society portrays and what people perceive. I've always been spiritually strong because when I found Jesus, He became this warm secure blanket that I found when my home was broken. He became my one solid thing. No matter what happens in this life, you can always count on your faith and the hope you cling to. One of the biggest inspirations of a life well lived as a shining example was Louis Zamperini.

Learning about and taking inspiration from other survivors is not only encouraging, but it can also help you through your own struggles knowing that someone went before you and came out on the other side. Louis Zamperini and many of the older veterans of my dad's generation were inspiring for me. Just look around and you'll find inspiration if your heart and eyes are open to it. Like a child, in their wonder, they fearlessly go exploring not giving thought to dangers because they just believe the world is their oyster and they're the kings of it. Sometimes, you have to approach life like that. Unlearning to learn is what I call it. You must unlearn some things to relearn and learn better.

What words of encouragement would you give to the 21-year-old Marilyn?

I would tell her, "It's okay. It was not your fault. Everything is going to be okay. You may not see it now, but you are blessed. There will be some rough patches along the way, but you'll get better, I promise. Jesus has some amazing things in store for you! Just wait and see!!"

Saying "Yes" to You

By Yesinia Vazquez-Rosa

Starting with Mindset

The success in my life has happened because of a few core things that we'll be talking about in this book. The power of empowerment, in the world of real estate, has made a huge difference in my life, and I'm now more interested in helping others find that equation in their lives.

As a child, I was told by my mom, "Dream big! Don't let anyone tell you what you can or can't do in life! Just, go for it!" She did her best to instill what I understood as the basics of a positive mindset in me. That optimism and hope, and the strength to keep going, and never giving up on your dreams.

My dad always instilled good thoughts and ideas in my mind, too. "Go to school. Do good. Be respectful." What was interesting was that my dad said different things to my brother. I know, in some ways, he was trying to protect me because I was a girl. I would have different expectations placed on me by society than my brother. I was to do what I was told. I was to say, "yes, sir" and "yes, ma'am." I was going to be a girl who would grow up to be a woman who would "fit in."

Honestly, I think that when my mom would, very strongly, pointing her finger at me with sternness in her voice, say, "Don't you EVER let someone tell you what you can be or do!," she was responding to what my dad was saying to me.

It was fairly early in my life that I realized I was different than the other little girls. I dressed differently. I saw things differently. I looked and talked differently. And, kids are punks sometimes, aren't they? So, I got bullied. I got picked on. Because I was different. Imagine a Puerto Rican girl in Tennessee, at the age of ten, in the 1980s. A brown, Spanish speaking girl in Tennessee. Let me tell you, it wasn't easy. It was a rough road.

My parents are ministers who chose Tennessee for their continued work. It didn't make any sense to me at the time. Why would we uproot our family roots to move from the beautiful island of Puerto Rico to the backwoods of a southern state like Tennessee? I had never heard of Tennessee, and it's not a place where immigrants dream of coming to when they dream of "America." But, this move, this change ultimately formed my strong identity and the strength I developed from being a Latina in a southern state. I now see as a tremendous gift from my parents.

I didn't come from money; I had very humble beginnings. I had daily run-ins with racist remarks, thoughts, and ideas about me. The mind plays tricks on you, so even at that age, you start to believe what people say and think about you, especially if it's negative. Oddly, you kind of shrug off good things that people say and think about you like they're not as important or true. But the negative stuff sticks like VELCRO®.

When a child is exposed to negativity like this, I think of "Charlie." Charlie isn't a real boy or girl, but a drawing of a little boy or girl, representing you or me, or some other small child. Perfectly drawn, smiling, and that paper he or she is drawn on is perfectly flat; no corners folded, or any creases or rips. But someone says something bad to that little child, and the page gets crumpled, as if in someone's hand, and they're balling up that piece of paper to be thrown away. Another insult thrown, and another crumple of the paper. A racist or sexist slur, more crumpling. And this goes on and on and on, until soon, that piece of paper is a crumpled up mess, fit only to "throw away."

But is "Charlie" the same? No. Those creases will remain. Maybe over time, they'll fade and smooth out. But they'll never be perfectly smooth again—those scars of discrimination, racism, sexism, and just plain bullying, never really go away. "Charlie" might still be smiling, but is he or she really?

Back when I was a child, my mind was playing tricks on me about whether or not I belonged. I would say to myself things like, "Why am I here? I don't belong here. No one likes me here. I dress differently than everyone else. I want to make friends, but I'm different and no one wants to be my friend." At that early age, that put things into my thoughts that made me think that maybe I wasn't worthy.

You have thousands and thousands of thoughts in a day, and sometimes you can't control those thoughts. So, I started feeling unworthy. I started feeling like crinkled up "Charlie." That no one really cared about me, and worse yet, didn't even really know I was there—that I wanted to be part of "them." I was a wadded-up piece of paper, and even though my mom and dad tried to help me out, it couldn't really do much against so much damage that was being caused within my own young brain.

As I got older, I realized that it's a big world out there, and I'm going to go make something out of myself. I decided that I wasn't going to let anyone tell me that I couldn't do what I wanted to do. And plenty of people told me I couldn't when I told them I was going to join the Air Force and leave Cleveland (where we were living, by that time).

In the Air Force now, over 20% of active-duty members are women. Back when I joined, that percentage was much lower—maybe half that many. By the time I joined, six women had served as pilots, co-pilots, or boom operators in 1986 during the raid on Libya. No one told those women, since 1947, that they couldn't be in the Air Force, so certainly no one was going to tell me that I couldn't join.

The Air Force taught me much of what I mean when I talk about mindset, and how it is much, much more than a "positive attitude," or "grin and bear it" type of philosophy. The Air Force, expectedly, taught me discipline and integrity, and what it means to show up—I mean, REALLY show up. There was and is no tolerance for "going through the motions" in the Air Force. You're either present 100% or you're not. It's that simple.

Through my military training, I developed physical strength, of course. But, more importantly, I developed mental strength and toughness. Skills that I have carried with me ever since. This strong mind, and the discipline behind that mental and emotional state further developed positive coping skills and being able to put up with just about any B.S. that might come my way.

When negative thoughts start to bubble up, certain skills that I was taught in the Air Force help me break out of that negativity in a way that helps me stand up taller and stronger. I no longer give into that negativity or listen to my own negative talk like I did when I was a "strange" Puerto Rican kid growing up in Tennessee.

What the Air Force taught me was to shut-down that type of negative noise. I look back at what I have accomplished, and start saying things to myself like, "I finished that last project on time, and it went great," or "I've achieved personal sales records during most years of my career—of course I can do this." The difference between those thoughts of the past and when they pop up now, is where they start.

When I get to that place of thinking, I can't do something, because of these external doubts that are turning internal, I tap into the coping skills that I've been taught and practiced throughout my life, but especially honed during my years in the Air Force, and since, personal development training and certifications that have added advanced tools. When I'm feeling those doubts, for instance, I'll ask myself, "Why am I feeling down on myself about this right now?" "What is my learning experience from this situation?" The key is on how quickly we can get back to center, to realign our inside voice and continue moving the needle forward.

It could be something as silly as not feeling pretty one day—that's something that we girls go through all the time—we are our worst critics in so many ways. Sure, sometimes I wake up in the morning and say, "Damn, you look fine this morning—you look great." Other days, I look in the mirror and think, "Ugh," and then remember my mindset—and my attitude changes, and I look back in that mirror: "You're amazing, you're stunning, and you are powerful."

According to the National Science Foundation, the average person has 12,000 to 60,000 separate thoughts, each and every day. Of those 60,000 thoughts, 95% repeat themselves—each. and. every. day. Worse? 80 percent of those repeated thoughts are negative – so 80 percent of those 95 percent of repetitive thoughts are NEGATIVE.

This creates neural pathways in our brain that make these thoughts super easy to have over and over. Think of a trail in a forest that has been walked on by thousands and thousands of people. It's wide, and smooth, and easy to follow because the pathway is well trodden. Compare that to a side trail that only a few people, maybe in the last week or so, have trekked on. This trail is much narrower, and sometimes you can't even see it—you hike along, and you lose the trail, and have to double back to get back onto the main trail.

These neural pathways are like these trails. If you think negative thoughts, 80% of your 95% of your repeated 60,000 thoughts, that path is going to be VERY wide and well-trodden. Let's do some quick math:

60,000 thoughts each day
57,000 (95%) of those thoughts are repetitive, AND
45,600 (80%) of THOSE thoughts are negative

Neural plasticity is what you're tapping into when you write, use, say and repeat positive affirmations. As silly as they might sound and feel when you do them, what you're building in your brain is a wider trail to offset the superhighway of negative thoughts that we're all naturally prone to. Our brain builds new pathways, or neural connections, for neurons (or brain cells) to travel. This is also what allows one part of the brain to do the work of a different part of the brain when that part has been damaged by injury or disease. So, it's not all fluff and circumstance when you practice positive self-affirmations—it's now understood to be scientifically applicable as we set on a path for creating a positive mindset.

Mindset also connects to your spirituality and emotional and physical health. What you focus on the most is what you will tend to bring into your life. That doesn't mean only good things happen if you're thinking only good things. But, when you can put your mindset into a positive and productive place, you can overcome negative things and people who might come your way. When you can command your thoughts instead of letting your thoughts command you, then you know you are in a better, stronger, empowered mindset.

Not that long ago, I was trapped in the corporate world. I would get up early, get myself ready, commute to work, make money for someone else, and commute home—exhausted. Every day, when I got home, I would think to myself, "Man, what am I doing? Why am I going there every day? It's not fulfilling me. I'm not able to be the creative person I know I can be." In that corporate setting, I couldn't really bring up my true value to the organization because it didn't fit into my "job description." Most of the time, when I would try to "stretch my wings" and bring my creativity into the job, an "executive" in the organization would block me—not seeing my value—not seeing the value that I brought to the organization—just seeing me as a threat, or someone to keep in "her place."

Every day I worried about how I was going to pay my mortgage.

How was I going to help provide for my family? How much I'm going to pay for food? I felt trapped. Not just in my own particular job but in this lifestyle that, for so many of us, is "normal." But is it normal to go through these motions, to just take a paycheck home? Is it "normal" to "do as we're told" so we can cash our limited income to pay our seemingly unlimited debt and financial obligations?

One day, I had this thought that would not leave my brain. That maybe there was an escape—a way out—that wouldn't threaten my home or my family. Maybe, just maybe, I could get off the "9-5" treadmill and make something for myself. The thing that finally "broke" me of thinking that I needed to stay stuck was that a supervisor decided to take my workout time away from me.

Let me back-up. For my lunch break, I was given 45 minutes each day. I would do a quick workout during my lunch hour, clean up, come back and have a quick lunch—all within the 45-minute break limit. I was told that I couldn't do that anymore because I couldn't "come back refreshed and ready for the afternoon meeting." On top of that, the afternoon meeting was being inexplicably changed to a different time that was going to interfere with my usual lunch break. It wasn't just going to affect me, it was going to affect several other individuals in the office who also used that time to go "off-campus."

I went home that night, exhausted as usual. But, I had thought about it, as I had been thinking about it for a while. I set my keys on the table, set down my coat, took my shoes off, and looked around. I had to do this. I sighed and sat down at the computer. "Dear Mr. X..." I typed up my resignation letter, printed it out, signed it, and brought it into the office the next day. On that morning's commute, I wasn't sure if I was going to do it. Was I going to really quit a six-figure job because I couldn't get my workout done during my lunch hour? Really? But, it was so much more than that. I had lost myself, and I needed to get back to who I knew I was, and what I knew I could become, and it just wasn't going to happen at this job. I felt like I was dying.

I walked into his office, letter in hand, and said, "Good morning, sir. I have something to tell you...I'm giving you my two-week's notice..."

I left a six-figure job because I just couldn't take it anymore. I gave up working crazy hours: 12+ each day. I gave up feeling like I was tied to my desk, to my chair. I gave up the feeling of not being valued. I gave up not being able to be creative and motivated. I gave up feeling like shit every day when I finally got home. I gave up a lot of money, yes, but I gained so much more. I gained myself back. I came back to life. I knew that I would rather gamble on me than gamble on an unhappy setting that doesn't serve me. Financially, yes, but internally? No.

I knew I could figure it out. I knew that if I had to eat peanut butter and jelly sandwiches until I got another opportunity, it's what I would do. I jumped without a net, but I said to myself, "I've got to go for it!" And holey moley, it's been a ride ever since!

And, I'm convinced this notion of mindset is what gave me the courage to walk away from something "great," into something truly limitless. Mindset gave me the power to empower myself. Mindset gave me everything I needed to start an incredible new chapter in my life. Mindset is what will guide you from leaving the military, corporate job, or any career shift.

Visualization of Your Perfect Self

I've always been a big dreamer ever since I was a little girl. Looking back, I can see that, even then, I would visualize things in my life that didn't exist, that later came to fruition. Today, I continue those journeys and visualize where I'm headed based on what I'm doing already. Even writing this for you, my reader, and experiencing this process of putting my thoughts and life-lessons on the page is something that I visualized quite some time ago. This practice of visualization has transformed my own life in ways that are almost impossible to define. In so many aspects of my life, I can see that I visualized things like speaking engagements, helping people to empower themselves, feeling abundance in my life, and so much more.

So, let's get specific on how this might look for you. What are some ways that you can bring visualization into your life. There are some tried and true techniques that go beyond the wishful thinking that I've referred to. The key is to go about practicing visualization deliberately, every day, throughout the day. Like the affirmations that I spoke about, this regular practice is what shifts things in your brain and also, in your heart. By opening up your realm of possibilities and seeing them play out in your mind on a daily basis, you're creating an incredibly effective imaginary space that can soon become reality for you.

Make Your Virtual Reality Real

When you are starting a visualization practice, you first must see what you see. This is not a generic vision. What do you see? Get specific. Really specific. Let's use a house as an example—maybe you see yourself living in your dream home. That's what we want to imagine. What does that dream home look like? How many square feet is it? How many bedrooms and bathrooms? What size lot is it on? How is it landscaped? Is it in a neighborhood, in the countryside, in a big city? When you walk into the home, what does it look like? What are the colors on the walls? How is it decorated? Do you have modern furniture? Retro furniture? What's the kitchen look like? How is your master bedroom decorated? What's in your master bathroom?

Your visualization will seem real when it feels real. The more details, the better. The more that you can really see things, the more you'll be able to move toward it, and see yourself there, in your home, through your eyes, walking around. As you strengthen those neural pathways with this vision of your dream home, you're increasing the chances that you'll take action toward your goal. That's how visualization works. It's not magic. It's action. It's action that YOU take, because you can literally SEE your life in your new dream home. It's right in front of you, and you'll do what you need to do to find yourself in that home.

Enhance the details involving all your senses, not just your eyes. What sounds do you hear as you walk through your dream home? What does the furniture in your living room feel like against your skin? What does the smell of the kitchen bring to mind—are you making cookies, baking a cake, preparing a huge Thanksgiving feast? Add more and more detail into what you're seeing and sensing until it's as if you're there and experiencing what you're visualizing.

Feel It

We all know that we make purchases not based on logic or reason. No matter how we would like to think otherwise, the vast majority of the decisions we make are based on one thing: emotions. We can do all the research we want on buying a new car, for example, but our emotions will justify any decision we make. When it comes down to it, how we feel about something almost always outweighs what we think about something.

Again, psychology informs us. In the world of cognitive therapy, we know that thoughts often come before emotions. How we think is often how we believe. For example, if we're watching a scary movie, and we see someone being slashed, we don't get too upset by it, because we know it's not real. Our knowledge, our thoughts, about what we know about the movie drive our emotions around it. We often think that it's the other way around: that our feelings drive our thoughts, but it's not. This is why when we change our thoughts (via affirmations, for example) we can change our feelings and how we respond to things in our life.

To make a visualization extremely powerful, we must add emotions to it based on what we know about our visualization. When we are walking in our new home, what are we feeling? Are we feeling pride? Happiness? Fulfillment? Do we feel at peace? What emotions are we having as we move from the street into the driveway? From the driveway through the front door? What are we feeling as we walk into the living room, into the kitchen, through the back door into the yard?

Once you can feel you're visualization—and I mean, REALLY feel it—you are in a new realm. Now you can move from seeing and feeling into DOING. You can take action toward what you're dream house is: what it looks like, how it feels, and the emotions that you feel in your dream home. You can even add a soundtrack to it all. Music is an incredible way to bring emotions up and out. Choose music that matches the emotions, and the intensity of those emotions, as you cross that finish line.

See Your Internal Vision, Outside

What you can imagine and bring forth is limited to what you have experience with, knowledge of, and what you've been exposed to. This isn't true for everything—of course, you can imagine something that you've never experienced—floating in space, for example. But, since visualization requires much more than just imagining, it is sometimes helpful to practice your internal vision, outside, in the real world.

Let's go back to your dream home. Have you ever been in a truly luxurious space? Maybe a luxury hotel, or a grand home during a tour of a mansion? In order to create a truly detailed version of your dream home, it can help to expose yourself to similar surroundings in the real world. You move from imagination to seeing how it could play out. You can see how things feel to your touch. What does a quartz kitchen countertop actually feel like, for example? How about a beautiful wool room-sized rug? What does that feel like? What does it smell like when it's new? How does a heated pool feel when you dip your toe into it? The more experiences you can give yourself in this manner, the more realistic your vision becomes. The more realistic your vision is, in your mind, from your perspective, the more you'll be motivated to achieve your dream.

Basically, what you're doing is adding data points. The more data you have about your new home, and how you'll feel in your new home, the more it seems real to you. For example, if you want to learn a new skill, like sailing a boat, you'll want to expose yourself to as many ways of experiencing that skill as you can. You'll want to read, watch educational videos, talk to people who have sailed, go sailing as a passenger, etc. Anything that increases your knowledge and gives you more data points through an awareness of what you need to do to learn to sail, you'll have a higher probability of seeing all of that through and learning how to sail a boat.

Now, you can visualize your dream boat, along with your dream home! And that's the key. Once you've visualized something to the point that you've achieved it, you need to ask yourself, "what's next?" This becomes your ongoing motivation for life, your "why." Your why isn't that dream home, actually, is it? No, your why goes deeper. It's a lifestyle. It's a freedom that that home represents. That dream home represents abundance, security and safety for you and your family. It's not a building. It's your "why," and seeing, feeling, and experiencing your why, every day, is what will get you there.

But, before you're "fit," you must put yourself out there. I remember when I told my parents that I wanted to be an entrepreneur. I sold my house, I quit my job, and both my parents went crazy. My Mom thought I was crazy, but I told her I would be ok. My Dad giggled when I told him that I would be the first millionaire that he knew. I said, "Watch me—you just watch." I had the confidence to achieve this. And, you must visualize that confidence in yourself, as well. When you do this, people will see that, and sense that, and line up behind you. With them, and with their faith in you, as well as your faith in yourself, things will come into your life that you have visualized.

When you put things out there, and you visualize, with intentionality, the universe will know when you're ready to receive it. Whether or not you believe in God, or think of this power as the universe, it doesn't matter. The energy is the same. When you're fit to receive what you visualize, that's when you will see it unfold in your life. Ask and you shall receive.

I visualized my life after the military, my life after the corporate world and I'm now actively living it out, creating and expanding my lifestyle, businesses, relationships, new opportunities, and my legacy. If you are not currently doing this in your daily routine, now it's a great time to start and experience the power of it.

Dream BIG

I think most people don't dream big enough. If you're dream isn't big enough, you will live in mediocrity. But big dreams come from being confident. Big dreams come from believing in yourself. Again, all of this depends on our mindset, from our earlier chapter. Dreaming big has been a part of my life since I was little.

When I was little, I knew I was going to travel the world. I shared with you my story of flying on Air Force Two for several years. I also had a dream of leading people and being an independent entrepreneur. I thought it, and I said it, and it came true. This goes back to our visualization section. By thinking it, and seeing it, and feeling it, you are more motivated to put your life into action to achieve those things.

The key thing is to dream bigger than you think you can achieve. My friends bring this up to me all the time, how I've said, "Hey, I'm going to be a Fortune 500 company someday—you watch!" All my friends, from many years ago, remember me saying that. It hasn't happened yet, but I wouldn't be surprised if it does. Life is about dreaming the impossible," and dreaming the "unreachable." Every Fortune 500 company started from nothing, but they weren't started by someone who didn't dream big.

Dreaming big is about not limiting yourself—thinking in a way that doesn't set limits on yourself and your potential. Thinking and doing life in a limitless way. Too often we limit ourselves because we think we can't do it. Now, with that said, that doesn't mean we should shoot for becoming a billionaire in one year. But we can dream big in the sense of living in abundance—the freedom to travel, to live in the house we want to, where we want to, pursuing what we want to.

Dreams sometimes fade away because life gets hard. We dream of a big mansion, and now we're 50, and we still don't live in that mansion. So, we throw our hands into the air and say, "Well, I guess I won't ever live in a mansion." Unless we train ourselves to deal with the curve balls that life throws at us, it's too easy to say, "I can't," versus "I can, and I will."

I know plenty of people who are way smarter than me. They are probably capable of bigger and greater things than the life that they're leading. But they give up at the first sign of difficulty, or they don't even see life as a dream. When asked, "What do you strive for, what do you live for," they would say, "I don't know…" Life is about going in circles to them.

I'm not judging. I've been there. We all have. It's those that step out of that lane, and forge a new path by dreaming bigger and seeing their life beyond its current state. Sure, I could make good money in the corporate world, but my potential there is limited. As an entrepreneur, I dream bigger. My potential for financial wealth is unlimited. My opportunity for abundance is unlimited. My potential to make a difference in the world, and in the lives of others, is unlimited.

When people try to stymie you—whether they are individuals, corporations, or governments—remember that your dream is yours, and it's yours to protect. So, as you take action on what you truly want to create in your life, keep it simple, command your mind, dive into your vision, take the action needed to move the lever, embody your core values in your leadership and commitment, and dream big, as you have one beautiful gift of life to create, make an impact, and leave your legacy.

Internal Surgery

By John Ready

There are times in your life that come to pass that really leave an impact on who you are going to be. You don't always know what those times are. You may not even realize the impact until years later. I relate a lot of my military experiences in this way. There are certain things that I will do, whether at work or home. When I think back, I realize that I made that choice for a reason. Many times, that reason is related to my military past.

I served in the U.S. Army (National Guard and Active Duty) from November 2001 to December 2009. I was at the recruiter's door on the first day they opened after September 11th. I always knew I would serve in some fashion. The attack on September 11th just hastened the process. I picked the Army to piss off my dad. He's a Marine vet. It just seemed right.

Growing up in a small central Kentucky town, I was excited to leave for basic training. I was ready to see the world. So, when my ship out day arrived, we took the two-hour drive down to Nashville for MEPS (Military Entrance Processing Station) to take my oath and head out. From Nashville, I hopped on a quick 45-minute flight to Louisville, KY, and took a bus down I-31W to Fort Knox. For reference, I could've walked to Fort Knox from my home (30 miles) in the time it took me to get there the way I did. But you know… The Government.

I volunteered for deployment to Iraq in 2003. This was an exciting time. We were training at Fort Campbell, KY (an hour from home), and were scheduled to deploy from Fort Campbell through Turkey in late spring. Late spring came and our deployment was cancelled. Turkey decided against letting us deploy across their border. So, I volunteered again in 2004. This time we were moved to Fort Dix, New Jersey, for rapid deployment. Yes, that Fort Dix. The same Fort Dix that was closed in the early nineties. And no, it was not a rapid process. But hey, I was out of Kentucky.

I spent the next 13 years out of Kentucky. And that is a part of this story. Because one of the things that they don't warn you about is the changes you have to make to yourself in order to make it in the "real" world. And I'm not referring to physical changes. That would have been too easy. That was something that we were accustomed to: making the physical changes to aid in the adaptation to our new environments.

No, the changes I was not ready for were internal... mental. That dreaded word in our world. Because we all thought that we were solidly in control of our mental health. I always "knew" that I could self correct any mental/emotional health concerns that would creep up. I had nothing to worry about.

With all of that said, there are three key adjustments that I wish I would have known about: support, mission-based mindset, and personal integrity. I know you are probably confused at what I mean by these three mental adjustments that don't entirely seem mental. Let me explain.

SUPPORT

Support. By any normal standard is an external factor, I get that. With veterans, especially newly minted veterans, support is a vital element. Support from your family. Support from your physical and mental health professionals—all external factors and all necessary for leading a normal, productive life. What veterans don't always have is a peer-level support system.

When a veteran first leaves the military, they don't think about the esprit de corps element that they are leaving. While serving, the veteran is immersed in a group of like-minded individuals who can share in the growth, successes, and even pains that the veteran goes through. This gives the service member a level of support that only a service member can know. And many times, take it for granted. This is something that the veteran may not immediately recognize as something that is missing. But if unprepared, it can have grave consequences.

This is the situation in which I found myself. I did not prepare myself for the lack of peer support—someone who can understand issues that I was going through. Someone who can help to carry that burden, to lighten that "load" I was carrying. I didn't have my military friends/peers there. I was half a country away from home, so I couldn't quite count on my childhood friends.

In essence, I was trying to carry a load that was too heavy for far too long. Over time I began to wear down, to let the load overwhelm me. I was over-worked. I had reached my breaking point, but with no external, peer-level support, I was left to fight this alone. Again, something that a service member doesn't have to contend with. This took me longer than I like to admit to figure out. But I eventually did.

The first thing I did was to join the veteran's affinity group at work. This gave me a group of people that had multiple things in common: work and military service. I had people that I saw on a regular basis and went through tough times with. This, on its own, was a huge measure. To know that I now had that external support that could understand and relate to, at least some of the issues I was facing, was world-changing for me.

The second thing I did, and with the support of my psychologist, was to investigate getting a service dog. It was a silly notion at first. In my mind, I wanted to not be seen, to sink back into the shadows and not have to worry about everyone else. I thought that a dog walking around with me would just add to the eyes that were on me. Needless to say, it took a while for me to open up to the idea. But I did. The application and training process, while tough, was very fulfilling. The dog, named MEMPHIS, was trained and provided by a small group in Wilmington, North Carolina. Their name is paws4vets. The dog has been the single biggest factor in keeping me grounded and level. I never would have guessed that sitting down and having a heartfelt, deep conversation with a dog could be as healing and refreshing as it is. At least with MEMPHIS, it looks like he understands what I'm saying and trying to process my words. And there's no judgment. I can lay everything out to him, and he'll still jump up into my lap without hesitation.

MISSION-BASED MINDSET

So, mission-based mindset is harder to explain. But it is the one that I struggle with the most. And, without the proper peer support, veterans can dig themselves into a deeper hole. As a veteran, some of us have been brought up that mission completion is paramount. Some missions being large and some small. But the "always place the mission first' mindset is always there.

This means that whenever something is going wrong, my relationship with my wife in this case, I try to fix it. For me, that meant digging into the only thing that I could control: my work. In my brain, I thought that the more I put my focus and attention into work, the better things would get within my family. Seems like an obvious mistake when looking at it from the outside, but when I was in the middle of it, I was lost. Grasping at straws, as it were. The only way I could make things better was to do my best in my work. So, as you can imagine, I made things worse. My family felt slighted, and I was adding tension to that by becoming more distant. When that was expressed by my family, I further dug in my heels and made things even worse. A bad cycle to be in.

With this backwards mission-based mindset and no one to help me through it, I was in a bad way. As I mentioned above, the support was a big part in fixing this. But the other part was adjusting this mindset. This meant that I had to do the very opposite of what I was doing. I needed to fully step away from the obsessive behavior which meant I had to step away from work. This was a very hard task, considering work was the sole thing I felt I could control and in fact needed to feel whole.

I had a path forward, finally. I sought out the supportive help I needed and stepped away from my work. This allowed me to pull the effort that I was putting into the work and focus it on the things that really mattered—my family. It wasn't perfect, but it was a start.

Personal Integrity

This one seems a bit weird, I know, but hear me out. When you think about integrity, you think about doing the right thing and being honest. And that is something that I lacked for a long time. Not that I was out doing the wrong things or committing criminal/immoral acts. Nor was I out lying and being deceitful.

Keep in mind, I was already in a bad spot. I was on the verge of losing my family. I had to step away from my work (which is what I dug into when I was struggling), and I was just having a really hard time functioning in society.

Before I had to step away from working, I continued to put on a strong face. I had to let everyone know that I was okay. Things were good. Likewise, at home I had to show that I was moving forward. Everyone saw through it but me.

Until I fully realized that the façade I was putting on wasn't for everyone else, but it was me trying somehow to convince myself that things were good. I was never going to figure out what was going on.

When I finally did start to figure things out and listen to what everyone else already knew, I started to see the lies for what they were. Just lies.

Putting them all together

So, I'm at my lowest. Trying to force each day. Losing my family. Destroying my career. I had to try something new. What I was doing wasn't working.

First, I started to realize where I actually was—admitting to myself that I needed help (Personal Integrity). Second, I started to reach out to those I thought I could relate to. I reached out to paws4vets and got started in their service-dog program for veterans (Support). Last, I started to retrain myself on the mindset that I was currently living in. I had to re-learn some things about failure and adversity and the different ways to address them, especially when they're internal (Mission-Based Mindset).

Where am I now? How are things? Thank you for asking.

My family is together, and we are back where this whole story began—back in Kentucky. I manage a large forging shop that manufactures automotive suspension parts. I'm happy. Do I have struggles? Of course, I do. I have had several missteps along the way. I've fallen back into holes that I thought I had climbed out of. It's easy to take some of the gains for granted. Especially to think a small victory can turn into winning the entire war. To get over-comfortable and lax. That's usually when life laughs at you and gives you a good wallop. To keep you honest.

I don't tell this story for sympathy or attention. I volunteered to tell my story in the hopes that someday it might help someone. Even if it's just one person, then I've accomplished a major goal. You see, I have had my help. Even when I didn't realize it, but it's been there. If I can pay it forward, then maybe the person that I help has that same opportunity to help someone down the road.

Thank you for taking the time to read my story.

I See Men as Trees

By Demetrius Booth

ORANGES FROM MAINE

> He spoke of trees, from the cedar tree that is in Lebanon even unto the hyssop that springeth out of the wall....
> 1 Kings 4:33

    The Gospel according to Matthew records a conversation that takes place between Jesus and a blind man. Jesus and the 12 disciples traveled to Bethsaida; a blind man was brought to him, and the crowd begged Jesus to touch him. Jesus takes the man by the hand and escorts him out of the village. It is there, away from the spectacle of the crowd, doubters, and naysayers that a remarkable conversation takes place. After spitting on the man's eyes and laying hands, Jesus asked him, "What do you see?" The man's initial response was, "I see men as trees." It is this conversation with Jesus that inspires the elements of this chapter. Trees are often used as an allegory for humanity in childhood fables, myths, poems, and Holy Scripture. It was my mother's loving touch on the eyes of my soul that shines through me, and I am all the better for it.

    I have heard, "Bloom where you are planted." In essence, what is being said is that you should be fruitful, no matter where we plant you. Based on deeply reflective conversations with my friend Joel Buys about trees, my views have changed. I have exhausted the top-rated internet search engine and couldn't find a single vendor selling oranges grown in a grove across Maine. Blooming where you are planted doesn't necessarily happen without massive amounts of labor to create the right conditions. Even then, location, environment, and climate matter. Chances are, you have never had an orange produced from a grove in Maine because the conditions are not prime for that tree to produce fruit there. "Bloom where you are planted" focuses all the responsibility for growth back on the person. Leaders must use the right tools at the right moment to set the right environment for their personnel to be fruitful. If you are leading in any capacity, look around at the trees in your organization…are the trees dead, suffering, languishing, coping, performing, or fruitful?

SOIL

> That you be rooted & grounded in love….
> -Ephesians 3:17

    We must choose to be fertile ground. My stomach is in knots...this is the great unknown. I have never felt fear like this. There is nothing that could have prepared me for this moment. My breathing is shallow. I notice it and consciously attempt to force air into my lungs. Nevertheless, regardless of how much oxygen I attempt to pull into my empty lungs, there just isn't enough. Not enough room, not enough days, not enough prayer, and not enough air to keep me from this intense moment of panic. I am living proof of surviving life with a broken heart, not because I wasn't prepared for this moment, but because I didn't like how my love had to leave this world. I pride myself on being able to change my destiny through sheer determination, discipline, and willpower. The softness of her voice echoes in the chambers of my heart; "be on the journey with me." For the first time in my life, it feels like this is happening to me instead of me making things happen.

    In the summer of 1999, I was in love with my high school sweetheart, so much so that I asked her to marry me and, less than 10 days after graduation, we were wedded. We are still driving each other crazy to this day. My mother was present at this small gathering that included my youngest sister Dominique and my now wife's cousin LaQuan. Second to the decision to spend the rest of my life with Lynette, I knew I had to provide a life for her, and that I could not do that at 18 years old on the south side of Chicago from my mother's apartment.

    I spoke with my Uncle George and stepfather about joining the Army. Both Army Reservists impressed upon me the quality of life I would experience by joining the Air Force and pointed me to a recruiter. In October of the same year, I walked through the "Gateway to the Air Force" in San Antonio Texas. The day I graduated from Basic Military Training, my mom was there watching her "Flyboy" being called an American Airman for the first time.

    The entirety of my existence has come to a screeching halt, but the world is spinning, and people are moving all around me. My empty screams fall lifelessly on the beach in the sands of time. In every moment, I am the culmination of many things—prayers of my ancestors, love of my family and the fruit of my mother's branch. The purpose of living is found along the journey of seeking. It is there on the path that you will find your treasure. I own this name; as a matter of fact, I inherited it. It belonged to my great-grandfather, my grandfather, my uncles, and my aunts. More importantly, my mother gave me this name.

That makes it mine. As far back as I can remember, my "aunty-team" has always said, "Your name will get there long before you do. Carry our family name with pride."

Recently I discovered that they claimed this wisdom from their mother, Annie Booth. A name is more than just letters strung together with thoughts, and syllables perched on our lips, more intuitive than vibrations of vocal cords. It's the embodiment of the soul. My beginnings were forged in darkness and crowned with glory. Spoken into life and giving way to the manifestation of my being, it's a declaration by the universe that I exist. Just as God spoke at the heralding of existence, and it was so. My mother gave life to me in this world by calling me her son. A seed planted isn't dead. It is in the place of struggling, striving, and strength.

The darkness of the wilderness is never meant to break you; the darkness was designed for you to break into yourself. The wilderness place prepares us for the calling to come. With tears in her eyes and a swelling of pride in her voice, my mother recorded a birthday message for me. In the most beautiful key, she sang Happy Birthday to her oldest child. There is a pause that catches me off guard. She tells the story of my birth from the most loving perspective—having long forgotten the pain of labor, the shame of being a single black mother, the difficulty of raising me (I have always been strong-willed), and the daunting task of preparing me for a world that did not yet exist.

The discovery that she had a son happened the moment the nurse placed me in her bosom. She recalled looking at my little face, my little lips, and my little eyes. The nurse asked her what she would name me, and her response was Demetrius Nathan Booth. It was at that moment she spoke into my life by proclaiming that I would be a man after her father's heart and that my life would honor him. My grandfather was my mother's hero.

(***Text sent; 2 June 2022 @ 17:17 CST***) *Hey Aunty/Uncle Team. We have made the final arrangements for Mom. It is her wish that her body be cremated. So, we have honored that and have arranged to have a Celebration of Life. Below are the details of the service, we are in the process of finalizing the flow. Once we have everything locked in, I will send you a note. An official message will come out soon, but I know you all need to start your planning.*

SEED

Some seed fell by the wayside, and the birds devoured it; some fell upon stony places and were scorched by the sun; some fell among the thorns and were choked. But others fell into good ground and brought forth much fruit.
Matthew 13: 4-8

True love requires that we give and make sacrifices because, without consequence, sacrifice is meaningless. Prayer is the transition statement for life. It spans all tenses...past tense, as it is backward-looking in thanks; present tense, as it allows us to enumerate our blessings; and future tense, as it grants us the courage to move towards the promise of God that awaits. The impact that you have on others is an indicator of the life you have lived. I have always taken the time to observe the world. My mother at this point in my life reminds me of my nature as I sit and watch her. I imagine like now, that I just wanted to take her all in. All the bad seems irrelevant as I consider the whole of who she is. The souls never die; their energy is transformed into something else that is beyond our understanding.

My mother was never one for keeping secrets. I would tell her that she was a pail with a hole in it. She would just smile and say, "Well." As the pancreatic cancer diagnosis was confirmed, she decided to attempt chemotherapy to give her children more time. She never wanted to do chemotherapy. One of her major concerns was it would crack the crown of glory that was her hair. Cancer is a devastating process; the journey is arduous for the patient, and it is helpless for loved ones. As the disease progressed and the chemotherapy was ineffective, she grew weaker. Moments of independence vanished as she needed help standing up, sitting down, and even going to the bathroom. At the time, unbeknownst to my younger brother Wesley and me, our mom began to hold the best secret. Domonique was the youngest of my mother's five children and was on her way toward marital bliss and is one of the most loving people created. In every moment, she is trying to figure out how she can do something for others.

This willingness to love others led to the best-kept secret that my mom never told. It was all planned out. Since my younger brother Wesley and I did not have the opportunity to do a formal mother-and-son dance because we didn't have traditional weddings. Domonique planned to yield the floor for us to do it at hers. At the time of the secret pact, only God knew that my mother's body would not make it to the day of the wedding. The secret was revealed only after my mother's passing. In a phone call to Domonique, just to check in on her, the details of the wedding came up. With a trembling voice and tears of anguish flowing, she told me what she and Mom were up to. "Mom and I had a secret, but I'm sure she already told you." We both laughed as I said, "Yeah, she probably did but what was she supposed to keep between y'all?"

Barely getting the words out due to the disappointment in the hand life dealt, Domonique replied "She was gonna dance with y'all at the wedding." It was at this moment that my mother's unintentional-intentionality shined through. Now, fighting back my tears, I proclaimed, "Man…that woman is something else." She had to have known and given Wesley and me tons of dances to make sure the plan came to fruition. During my visits home to take care of my mother, she would move back and forth as my hands supported her weight while helping her stand or sit, getting in and out of the car, or going to the bathroom. I would ask, "Are you trying to dance with me," and she would reply, "Umm hmm." Without knowing, I was complicit in her plan to gift me hundreds of dances. It was only later that Wesley revealed that he would play music during the chemotherapy sessions and the two of them would two-step.

My mother's gifts to her children were planted as seeds of love. Even in the moments when she was less than perfect physically, despite trauma and hurt, she found a way even in her passing to teach life's most important lesson. With unintentional-intentionality love was sown because that's all that could be found in the soil of her soul, and we are the fruit of it.

ROOTS

We are pressed on all sides, but not crushed; perplexed, but not in despair; persecuted, but not abandoned; struck down, but not destroyed.
-2 Corinthians 4:8-9

Two years after serving the Air Force, the horrific events of September 11, 2001, happened, and the United States military was mobilized for the GLOBAL WAR ON TERROR. After multiple deployments to some of the most inhospitable places in the world, and the devastating effects that it had on me spiritually and mentally, I had built a sense of resilience that couldn't be taught. I would have to call upon those elements during one of the most arduous journeys of my life.

Every day you show up is a testament that you haven't given up. One of the most solemn moments I have experienced was helping my mother complete her paperwork after the initial oncology appointment. Sitting next to her and my sister Domonique in the chair across from me, with Quianna on Facetime. She was pregnant and with the world still reeling from the effects of the global COVID-19 pandemic, it was decided that the best thing was for her not to come to the doctor's office and put herself and the babies at risk. When it was time to fill out the portion regarding the DNR wishes of my mother, I became overwhelmed with emotion.

A Do Not Resuscitate (DNR) document is the most arduous act of love on a journey like this. It requires you to put the needs of your loved one above personal desire. I know it doesn't feel like it, but that's the surface of this moment, and the negative voices of judgment in our heads. It hurts, and you question yourself. Your love and desire to protect them from the worst in life is what helped you come to this place. Keep showing up; make being present a priority, and care for yourself and others who are joining you on the journey. The first step to being courageous and holding on to hope is showing up!

I remember looking back at her and wondering what she was thinking and how this was impacting her, and, at the same time, I could not stop the floodgate of tears that poured forth. This was the first time that I had to consider existence without my mom. It's not lost on me that everyone dies. This happens to be the cycle of living in our fallen world. But for the first time, I was met with my mother's mortality in the form of a sheet of paper and her wishes not to be connected to tubes or experience the consequences of the process of having her body brought back to the medical terms of life. I could barely get the words out, in an attempt to comfort her, which, as I look back in hindsight, were more for me.

"I am going to be okay; it's just I love you so much and this moment is overwhelming me, and I can't stop the tears. So, I will do the paperwork as I go through this." Then I asked if she was okay, I was only met with a head nod, affirming she was. Domonique was already in tears and seeing me hurting caused her to hurt more. Research has surfaced outlining that if trees grow in an environment where they don't have to withstand wind resistance, their roots will not develop properly, and eventually will succumb under the pressure of their own weight.

The process trees go through is called building "stress wood". The lack of "stress wood", which is a critical element as trees grow, helps the tree become stronger. Without it, the trees can't thrive. The wind that comes in the form of resistance is vital for the tree to flourish and emerge as it was designed. You may have heard pressure makes diamonds. In the same way without the resistance of obstacles and difficulties, we wouldn't develop properly. Don't complain about the trial—you are being tested so God knows what's in your heart.

I am convinced that hope requires courage. Every day you stand, you are being strengthened. Every moment you don't quit, you are growing stronger. Each time you come back, your resolve deepens, and your roots spread deeper. I often think back to that moment; it felt as if the force of the wind was going to cause me to topple. All the while, I was developing "stress wood" that would allow me to stand amid the storm on the journey to come.

(Text sent; 2 June 2021 @ 20:28 CST) *Hey Aunty & Uncle Team. Mom has been diagnosed with Pancreatic cancer (ductal adenocarcinoma) which is the most common form. This message is intended to ensure we keep y'all in the loop as we all start this journey with Mom.*

LIGHT & LOVE

Nothing For My Journey Now

Conflict is the Crucible for Character. My heart is broken, and I am not sure I want that to change. I don't want this pain to hurt any less; I want to feel this, and I don't want this heartache to end. I will continue to live, but somehow the thought of enjoying life without you doesn't seem fair at all. These were the words echoed from my soul and were written in the margins of a page of a book I was given. I define grief as the deepest expressions of love that have been stored up for a specific person with nowhere to go. Nothing is either found or lost. I believe we subconsciously place things so that we can come back to or call upon them when we need them most. It is a token left by us as a reminder of our strength and purpose.

We are set on a path to remember through our experiences. On purpose, with purpose, and for a purpose I found myself in Chicago. There was this moment during a Duo video call with my mother when I noticed she was not in high spirits. My question, "Should come home?" was met with a head nod, because she could not muster words. I spent those nights on the floor next to her bed. There were instances when she forgot I decided to sleep there next to her, and when she would call for me, I would startle her. During one of the days present with her, I noticed that she had started to drift in thought. I called her back to me and asked where she had been. "Thinking about home," as she looked back at me with those hazel-colored eyes.

"What's waiting for you over there," I asked. "My daddy, Nathaniel Booth, my mother Annie, Joe, Margaret, George, Tony, and Billy Ray." She paused in thought, "You don't know them yet, but you will when you get there… and Greg." This list of souls were the parents and siblings that had preceded her to eternal life. "And Jesus, Jesus will be there. You know what I want when I get there." With my heart in my throat, I responded with "No ma'am, what do you want?" "For Him to say, "Well done, my good and faithful servant.""

"Nothing for my journey now." These words carry a deeper meaning for me now. The reason there was nothing for my mother to carry on the journey during the last year of her life is because the seeds she planted produced a bountiful harvest. She didn't need to bring anything for the journey because the people who accompanied her brought everything she needed from this point forward. "Just be on the journey with me." Everyone showed up in their own way. I will capture some of the offerings presented by her children, but know that her husband, sisters, brothers, daughters-in-law, sons-in-law, grandchildren, nephews, nieces, lifelong friends, church family, and pastor all brought gifts of love to help along the way. My mother had five children that sprang forth from her womb and one that was grafted in. It is from this perspective I offer light and love.

In the wake of my mother's passing, the youngest of us carried the heaviest weight. Domonique had worked a full-time job and spent most days taking care of Mom post-shift. Of note, she worked 12-hour shifts at a hospital. Her elements of love took the form of **Caregiving**, **Comfort**, and **Protection**. She delved deep into reflection as she expressed her gift of wanting to be the caregiver in the way Mom was for everyone else. With tears in her eyes, she thought back on the comfort she provided, as Mom endured procedures, and the protector came out during times when Mom couldn't speak up for herself or express what pain she was experiencing.

Mom would often affirm with Charlotte that she was a good mother. Those seeds sprung forth as she strived to offer her special gift. Charlotte used her motherly instinct to ensure **Comfort** and **Dignity** were never lost. As you can imagine, as an adult not being able to hold your drink of water, stand by your strength, or wipe yourself can be damaging. "I always made sure Mom never lost her dignity, even when she had an accident and would be so apologetic as I wiped her; I would remind her that she was loved and that it was ok. So, she never felt shame." Quianna's offering of love during Mom's last year with us brought a harvest of **Rest** and **Joy**. "The rest came in the form of I didn't want Mama to have to worry about anything. No stress about bills getting paid, working the schedule for doctors' appointments, paperwork, and applying for social security and disability. We all know I understood the assignment and gave Mom twins. My gift of joy came from Cailey and Caicey." My mother was number 8 of 16 children and happened to be a twin at that. We would all argue about who was Mom's favorite. I believe this was the thing that blessed her soul the second most. Once Cailey and Caicey arrived there was no question that they were her favorite. Wesley is confident in his purpose on the journey, and so is everyone else. As I gathered the individual stories, everyone commented that they believed Wesley would say "laughter". He was the in-house comic relief growing up. There is no situation that he is going to take too seriously. I always hear him say, "Life is too serious all the time; we need to laugh." With an overwhelming sense of love, he proclaimed, "I brought **Laughter**, **Trust**, and a **Listening Ear**. Laughter has always been my position and how I loved her. Trust in the sense that she respected the man I have become, and that means the world to me that she entrusted her health to me and honored my service to her." My purpose is to be a nurse and take care of people based on my experience and expertise. She would come to me and tell me what the Doctor said and speak with me about it. A Listening Ear: When I took her to chemotherapy I would ask about my father and manhood. She would tell stories so fluid and real to offer me a perspective of not just who he was but who she became. Through all the tears, pain, and hurt she deserved to laugh to help her forget cancer even for a moment. Even as she was dying, she poured more love into us. Cory is the son who was grafted in. Between all of us, we joke that I am mom's firstborn, but Cory is the oldest child. In the wake of his father-in-law's transition to eternal life and the support, he learned to give to his wife Demekia. He purposefully brought intentional moments to deposit an environment of love along the journey. If you asked him, he would consider his contributions as small tokens to offset our collective efforts. The truth is, surrounding her with positivity made life all the richer. Demeika has this instinct to love, "Sometimes you don't know what you need," is the proclamation written on her heart that informs the recipient that they are in a showering of care. With her blessing and sometimes instructions, Cory would fly into town every third month to take Mom to chemotherapy. One time he brought her a beautiful basket of healthy snack options that we all credit Demeika for (he still claims he did it on his own…no one believes that). My mother never ate any of that healthy stuff. She preferred Pepsi, but she would show that basket to everyone. Good love will do that to you; it will put a pep in your step, a smile on your face, and hope in your heart. The token he brought was hope, and hope does not disappoint! My offering on the journey was a **Reminder to Look Up** and **Connections to Love**. During her stay with me in 2022 while I was stationed at Columbus AFB, she had a very tough moment. I helped her to the bathroom, and I am not sure what it was that caused the fracture, but she cried out in anger to God. "I asked you to heal me and to help me." After she yelled it the third time, I responded with "Look up." As she looked up at me, I reminded her that while the answer to healing may have been no, God sent you tons of help. If you are ever in question of that all you need to do is look up and you will draw strength because you are going to see me, Cory, Wesley, Quianna, Charlotte, and Domonique. If you ever feel down, all you need to do is…her response, "Look up!" It was time for me to bring my mother back home. I had played the long game and coordinated ahead of time for her to be with me. Unknown to my siblings, it happened to fall during Mother's Day. My mother thought that was the funniest thing, that none of them paid attention to the dates that she would be with me. As I knelt putting on her right shoe, she tapped both sides of my shoulders with her hands and said, "Y'all really did love me." Dismissive at first, I responded, "Yeah check, we love you…you loved us first. We still owe you some love." Continuing my task of getting her ready, as I placed the left shoe on her foot, she tapped my shoulders again with both her hands and in the most loving voice repeated, "Y'all really did love me!" This time, I paid attention; looking at her in those green eyes, I reverted to the eleven-year-old kid who just wanted her to be okay. "Yes ma'am, we love you. We always have. You loved us first, and it's impossible not to give some of that back." She smiled and responded with, "Umm hmm, I know." Those were some of the last words my mother said to me before she transitioned. We continue the journey to discover what other treasures await us that she left behind. My mother needed nothing for her journey because the fruit of the seeds she planted brought forth—caregiving, comfort, protection, dignity, rest, joy, laughter, trust, a listening ear, hope, a reminder to look up and connection to love.

D's Life Lesson

1. Resilience is the precursor for strength. It doesn't come from a workshop, seminars, or internet video. It comes from weathering life's storm—whether by walking, crawling, standing, or on a knee. Resilience is always viewed on the other side.

2. Not everyone comes equipped with the Tensile Strength to hold you together, lift you, or carry you through the worst parts of life's

journey. Some people are there for a season, understand that, and when the season is over, let them move on.

Love In an Unexpected Place

> God is in this place, and I didn't know it.
> Genesis 28:16

I dedicate this section to the people who stopped for me. In holy scripture, God is expressed as the manifestation of love. At any point, you feel or experience it, it's because God is nearby. In the wake of my mother's passing, I experienced some of the worst moments of my life. As the world continued to spin and life moved on for everyone, I noticed when people stopped for me. It came in when I expected it the least. My dear friend Niecee would pray for me, and when the spirit of God led her, she would call or text just to check-in. I never expected dad jokes to be something to lift my spirits; Tanner (T-Dog) Barber, and Daniel (Slim) Seifert always stopped in to ensure I smile every morning, and T-Dog gave me a gift that changed my life.

Donald Staats would come by to share stories about his father, ensuring I knew I was never traveling alone. Bradley Bell would remind me of the strength I have and the people who wanted to give back to me, because I cared for them. Michael Olson was one of the most genuine human beings I have ever met. He cared for me in a way that I never expected, and purposefully saw me and opened his heart to suffer with me. My Aunty/Uncle team, cousins, Branch 21 (Cory, Connie, Camille, Ira Jr., Demeika, Rika, John, Wesley, Quianna, Charlotte, and Domonique) you mean the world to me, and your kindness strengthened my soul. How fortunate to be held together by people who had nothing to gain...they loved because that's what was in their souls.

Georgia A. Booth-Price, I look forward to seeing you when I transition to the other side. Until then, I am going to work and make the most of these moments of life that you have given me. I can't wait to talk with you about what I did with it.

Destiny Calling: Warrior of the West Side

By Jeffrey Hall

This superhero's story begins on Chicago's West Side in some of the poorest neighborhoods, including several housing projects. The primary objective was survival because peril lurked around every corner. Looking back, it is clear that I have been destined for a life of service, caring for others, and leading others, from the very beginning. Every experience, every challenge, every heartbreak, and every encounter has been necessary and has led me to where I am now. Despite the pain, I have few regrets; it has all been worth it.

In my early urban environment of "survival at all costs", where peril lurked around almost every corner, I am not ashamed to say that I am here to tell this story because of some of the most amazing women I have ever known. These women were my Granny, mom, aunt, big sister, and three first cousins. These women were intelligent, loving, compassionate, and ever vigilant. Nothing was getting past them! They were fierce warriors in many regards. They also carried significant pain and unresolved issues from their past, including hurts passed on for generations. They did their best with what they were working with, and somehow made it work. Growing up so closely involved with them, they each profoundly influenced me.

There were also positive male role models that, in retrospect, had more influence on me than I realized before. My older brother—now a professor and Ph.D.—was always passionate about education. My great uncle, Granny's big brother, was a Major in the Army during World War II and married a woman he rescued from a concentration camp. He was a huge role-model for me. Three of my mom's ex-boyfriends served as Marines in Vietnam, and I recall learning some of their stories, which always fascinated me. There were also stories of two uncles who both served in Vietnam as Marines and met their end on the streets of Chicago shortly after returning home.

These amazing people had a hand in shaping the man I would become, but Granny was by far my most considerable influence. Granny is my superhero and my most influential role model. She embodied love, compassion, selfless caring for others, service, strength, and intelligence. She held the family together and inspired us all. Granny is also a published author of multiple poems, and her ***West Side Story,*** tells of her family's exodus from Bogalusa, LA, to Chicago's West Side in the 1920s. Of her six grandchildren, I spent the most time with her.

These incredible women made a huge difference in every part of my life, not only in relationships. They inspire me in every way and are part of my outcome. Their influence and examples, combined with my early inner drive and desire to have and be more, have piloted my course in the quest for love, acceptance, and success.

As I write this, I am still working to make sense of it all, and if you are willing to be patient enough to take this expedition with me, we will all come out on the other side a bit better.

From my earliest memories, there were always many challenges that are, looking back, far from average or everyday by definition. Besides having a single-parent mom suffering from depression and other issues while struggling to raise four children, there was never enough of anything through resources—money, food, etc. Even toilet paper, dish soap, and bathing soap were luxuries for which we often were forced to find creative solutions.

We stretched the imagination when it came to finding substitutes for toilet paper, and Granny would save the day by making soap for every possible use from goose grease and lye. Our food stamps never went very far, mainly because our mother did her best to buy food that was as healthy as possible but was more expensive. My brother and I also had voracious appetites.

The project's community gardens provided one opportunity to keep hunger at bay. We didn't have one of our own, but we often did some midnight harvesting from our neighbors' gardens as a family. My mom and older brother would crawl through the gardens in the middle of the night, dressed in black and toting garbage bags for the loot, while my older sister and I would assume the lookout duties. My baby sister had not yet arrived, and I was between preschool and first grade at the time of these escapades. Thankfully, we also received provisions from food pantries, for which we were extremely grateful.

As far back as I can remember, my mom never held a steady job. Only the occasional part-time gig at a neighborhood grocery or fast-food joint, and these were very few and far between, which was very likely due to the mental issues that haunted her, leaving her severely depressed, largely immobile, and incapacitated for long periods, and effectively incapable of being a responsible, nurturing parent and breadwinner. So, the four children stepped up when needed to assume these roles, essentially raising ourselves and each other, which often meant we were responsible for finding creative solutions to absent resources.

As I mentioned earlier, we did live in some of the poorest neighborhoods in the city, so our woes did not end with the short supply of food, soap, and toilet paper. Safety was a constant battle, especially in the high-rise projects where the elevators rarely worked, the stairways were often dark, gangs were rampant, addicts were desperate, pimps were looking to recruit fresh talent to fill their stables, and kids who likely experienced some form of abuse at home tried their hand at bullying. The police were scared as hell to enter. Oh yeah. There was also the never-ending battle with rats the size of Chihuahuas that we would have to beat to death with a bat, because the poison was a snack, and rat traps only slowed them down and pissed them off.

When I was nine years old, my little sister was born, and shortly after that, my older brother and sister left. My brother went to college, and my sister got pregnant and married by age sixteen. This event was tough on me for many reasons. My brother was moving to what may as well have been another planet, and I had no way of knowing when or how often I would see him after being together every day for all these years.

My sister's departure, however, was far more traumatic for me. We were very close; the day she left was sudden and forced. She was pregnant and almost due to deliver when she physically challenged my mother, and they battled violently. At that moment, I was terrified, frozen, and had no clue what to do. Mom ordered me to call the police, and I don't remember much after that.

With just the three of us now in the home, this meant that I would have to step up big time, and at the age of nine, I became the parent on duty for my infant sister and the man of the house. This new role involved all of the domestic responsibilities you would assume came along with it and so much more. My mother routinely placed demands on me that were unsafe, unethical, illegal, and sometimes life-threatening. She did not appear concerned about anything other than getting what she wanted.

By the time I was in my second year of high school, I had stopped counting the number of times we moved. We had also been homeless several times, as my mother prioritized prescription meds and sending money to a tele-evangelist over paying the rent. While I enjoyed learning and absorbed much while in classes, school became a luxury I could no longer afford, as far as time was concerned. Survival and taking care of the household were higher on the list of importance at the time, so I dropped out in my sophomore year.

It would take more chapters to paint a picture of the responsibilities and pressure dumped on me, and the unbelievable situations in which I often found myself. The expectations, the utter lack of remorse and accountability my mother levied, and the potency of her venom was nothing short of remarkable. There were moments when I slipped into depression and despair when I even contemplated suicide.

In the winter of 1980, as I was preparing to enter high school, I nearly broke down after we lost our apartment and belongings in a fire and found ourselves homeless again. I could genuinely feel myself losing it. My mother took me to the hospital emergency room where they asked me questions that caused an alarm within. Without fully knowing what immediate or long-term impact my responses would have, I just had the impulse to pull it together and say whatever I needed to say to get out of there and go home, which I did. For a time, I managed to suppress these overwhelming emotions successfully.

At around age seventeen, we moved into a charming three-bedroom, rent-subsidized apartment in a great racially diverse neighborhood on the city's far north side. Some parts of life improved. Some got worse. It was here and at this time that I landed my first real job. It was in telemarketing, and I quickly excelled, getting promoted to supervisor in my first month on the job. I was earning some decent money and starting a social life, and my confidence was rising.

At this time, my mother dialed up the knob on the mental, emotional, and verbal abuse to unbearable levels. So, I began planning my departure by opening a bank account and saving money for my first apartment, which I would move into right after my eighteenth birthday, following a final verbal assault from her. The confrontation was on a Tuesday night, and I was in my new apartment by that Friday.

Everything changed completely and became a transformational point that would tremendously impact who, what, where, and how I am today. As I reflect upon this, it was the first time I acknowledged my worth and stood up for myself in this way. This fight was far different from the brawls I had on the streets for physical survival. This fight was for my mental and emotional survival, as well as for my dignity.

Shortly after moving out, I took night General Education Development (GED) classes at a community college and soon earned my "Good Enough Diploma". Education was vital to me, and I enjoyed learning. I also knew I would only get so far without at least a GED.

Not realizing that part of my conditioning led me to be a caregiver, it wasn't long before I found myself in a family situation similar to the one

I had fled a little more than a year before. At my job, I met, courted, and rescued a single mother of a one-year-old daughter in a desperate situation. Mere weeks after the start of the relationship, they were living with me in my studio apartment, and I again was caring and providing for a family.

Roughly a year into this arrangement, the telemarketing company where we both worked shut down abruptly, and we lost our jobs with no warning and no severance. Finding anything with pay comparable to what I had been earning seemed impossible, and the financial situation was becoming more and more desperate.

After working several jobs that led nowhere, including doing telephone surveys and working as a collector on defaulted student loans, I decided to join the Navy. This decision was motivated mainly by my desire to provide long-term security and benefits for my new family, not just a regular paycheck. The recruiter informed me that my Armed Services Vocational Aptitude Battery (ASVAB) score of fifty afforded me one of two career opportunities in this fine establishment. My choices were cook or corpsman (the Army and Air Force have medics). Having already decided that I would be staying for at least twenty years and that this was indeed a career, I accepted for the long haul. I opted for corpsman because of the variety of long-term options this path would provide. In November 1987, I married for the first time and went to basic training in Great Lakes, IL, the next month.

It was extremely tough at the beginning of my Naval career financially. I spent the first two years in Great Lakes, IL. These two years included boot camp, Naval Hospital Corps School, and an official assignment to Naval Hospital Great Lakes. Financial hardship was the primary reason for getting orders so close to home. The marriage also soon began to suffer and slowly unravel. However, it would take a few more years, a deployment to Operation Desert Shield/Operation Desert Storm with Third Battalion, Six Marine Regiment, and two more duty stations before I decided to walk away. There was more of that familiar anger, hostility, and lack of connection that hurt so deeply and eventually became unbearable. I had to go for sanity, safety, and peace of mind. This parting of ways ripped me apart, for I wanted this to work.

During this time, I started taking college courses with the plan of chipping away at a degree little by little to prepare for professional life after the Navy. The Navy also offered various correspondence courses that I took advantage of regularly. While I did not aggressively pursue advancement in rank early on, I was an avid reader and continued to grow in other ways. There was limited time for these activities because I moonlighted quite a bit when home between deployments. The pay was not great, and I continued to provide financial support for my ex despite our being apart.

Several years after separating from my first wife, I met who would soon become my second wife. We will call my second wife-to-be Princess, a nickname her mother affectionately called her in Korean. Princess was also a single mother; she had a two-year-old son and a compelling damsel-in-distress story that moved me to be the rescuer and caregiver again.

This marriage lasted longer than the first, but it would also come to a painful end. Despite all the turmoil and issues that could have been a distraction, I remained laser-focused on pursuing advancement and higher education. I earned the honor of getting promoted to Chief Petty Officer.

The path to promotion to the coveted rank and title of Navy Chief (E-7) in the highly competitive rating of Hospital Corpsman requires next level dedication, planning, and sacrifice. It is anything but easy, and there are no shortcuts. The selection board considers your cumulative contribution to the Navy, your command, Sailors and Marines in your charge, collateral duties, off-duty education, community service, and deployments to austere environments. The board also heavily weighs your test scores on the Navy-wide Advancement Examination for Chief Petty Officer and several years of fitness reports (performance evaluations).

My serious planning to make Chief began when I was a Petty Officer Second Class (E-5) while stationed at Third Medical Battalion in Okinawa, Japan, with my second wife and stepson. Following the priceless advice of a seasoned lady Navy Chief, I polished turds. By this, I mean I assumed roles and responsibilities no one else wanted and delivered results beyond all expectations. I was diligent in documenting them in my fitness reports. Pushing my mind, body, and spirit to the limits, I volunteered for every tough assignment and deployment I could get; I spent countless sleepless nights studying and preparing for online college courses, Navy correspondence courses, warfare designations (Fleet Marine Force, Surface Warfare and Air Warfare), and advancement exams. Because of my desire to bring others along with me despite the competition, I also prepared training materials for others seeking advancement and pursuing warfare designations. Of course, I documented everything I did to help myself and others in the package I prepared for the selection board that would eventually determine my worthiness to wear the Chief's uniform.

The most significant event leading to my road to Chief was my eight-month deployment as a member of Fleet Surgical Team Seven of Expeditionary Strike Group Seven/Task Force 76 (Amphibious Force U. S. Seventh Fleet) 2004/2005. During this deployment, we supported operations in the Battle of Fallujah that stretched the capabilities of our team and the resources of the ship's medical department, treating casualties from various field operations. Following the tsunami, we provided humanitarian relief to Indonesia and conducted a medical and dental civil action project in economically devastated East Timor, where we witnessed poverty beyond imagination. During this deployment, I also lost my closest cousin to suicide but could not fly home to attend services and support my family.

I want to point out that amid all this hard work and sacrifice, my marriage was a battlefield with daily turmoil, pain, bitterness, and confrontations that did not dissipate with geographical separation. My home life had no shortage of distractions and excuses for me to quit. Yet, with every ounce of negativity I received, I was even more determined to serve with distinction and reach my goals. Some helpful coping strategies I developed to get me through this deployment successfully included some counseling sessions with the ship's chaplain, regularly attending services and Bible study, working to improve the morale of my fellow Sailors and Marines, laser-focus on the mission, and a tremendous amount of time devoted to personal and professional development.

In July 2005, all of this hard work and sacrifice paid off; the news was delivered by a brief phone call from one of my Chiefs, congratulating me and giving me orders of where to report the following morning for the beginning of my six-week training phase which would adequately prepare me for this monumental role.

The next six weeks would be the most demanding, educational, and transformational period of my Naval career. This final path to donning the uniform and wearing the coveted anchors forever transformed me as a leader. From this point, I embraced the idea of leadership by example and would aspire to a reverent leadership style.

Upon retiring from the Navy, I landed a corporate sales job where I again excelled quickly. I completed my B.S. in healthcare management at Northeastern University, while working insane hours, completing most of my assignments in airports and hotels across the country. After two years, I left (on excellent terms) to pursue my M.S. in Health Informatics at the same institution.

There were two more failed marriages between leaving the Navy and halfway through completing my graduate degree—the fourth activated dormant mental and emotional issues which derailed me significantly. Momentarily incapacitated, I would have to return to finish my degree some years later. Again, I found myself homeless, sleeping in my car with my dog, Larry. This time, I chose homelessness, leaving a toxic environment to find peace and figure out how to move forward with my life.

This period was make-or-break and could have gone either way. It was also the darkest and most precarious time when I was angry and constantly engaged in risk-taking behavior that could have ended my life at any moment. However, I still made time to volunteer and serve on the boards of local non-profits that served the community, and I still pursued opportunities in business.

My brutal truth at this moment was that, until I became aware of, confronted, and received care for the issues holding me back—like posttraumatic stress disorder (PTSD) and others—I would not lead a productive life. So, I did, and I am now living a very abundant life.

The saving grace that helped me through this scary time was an inpatient program at the Veterans Administration (VA) hospital. Here, I had the opportunity to reset and effectively address the issues hindering me, in a supportive environment with my brothers and sisters, who were experiencing much of what I was and had been going through. Broken and lost, I fully committed to the program, embraced every lesson delivered, and set goals for my new future —many of these goals I have already achieved.

My cumulative experiences and challenges led me to a life of service and caring for others in many ways through service to my country by caring for the sick and wounded, care and compassion for the poor and homeless, people suffering from mental health issues, and those who have been abused and neglected.

If anyone were to ask me if I would go back and change anything in my past, given the opportunity, I would not. Although many events in my history were painful and challenging to navigate, every experience contributed to the man I am today, and all I have come to enjoy. Without the events that have shaped me, it isn't easy to imagine what type of person I would be today.

The transformational moments are many, and each has made me stronger, wiser, and more capable. Each has given me tools I can share with others for their betterment. I have a few personal takeaways in my approach to life, love, and the pursuit of professional and business success.

Three superpowers in my arsenal have helped me overcome the seemingly impossible, strive, and pursue a path of continuous self-improvement in every way. Faith and courage, an intense drive to help others, and a fierce determination to break unhealthy cycles are the superpowers to which I attribute my success.

Faith and courage I group together because they have proven mutually exclusive and powerfully effective for me. They have helped me embrace the unknown and overcome those things that would have otherwise held me back. They caused me to push myself to march forward when I wanted to give up. The belief that my environment and circumstances neither define nor limit me, that no person can tell me what I am not capable of, and a knowledge that I can consistently achieve and be more is a result of faith and courage. They have led me to be the confident and competent person I am today.

Faith is my belief that I will overcome despite the bleak circumstances. This faith is fueled by my personal history of somehow surmounting the insurmountable many times with the help and guidance of the Divine. This faith makes it possible for me to face fear head-on and ignore the words of those who say that I cannot or am not enough.

Courage, by the way, is not the absence of fear but carrying out what you know must be done in the face of it. More times than I can count, I experienced intense fear; times growing up when I had to fight someone larger than me or more than one person at a time, deployment to combat and other missions, where the outcome was far from certain, facing the uncertainty of homelessness on multiple occasions, and many other situations in which I found myself at various stages of my life. These were dark and scary moments where I had no way to predict the outcome or even my chances for survival. However, running away or giving up quite simply was not an option, nor was I accepting that any of these moments would end my story. In these moments, I would think to myself that I have come through worse, and so have others.

Being a caretaker has always been a huge part of who I am, and I have always had the innate drive to be of service to others in whatever way I was capable of, using whatever resources I had at my disposal. These tangible and intangible resources often involved giving a big piece of myself. It can be easy to surrender to debilitating worry and throw intense pity parties when life looks grim. It is incredibly therapeutic to help others in similar or greater need during these times. Doing so has distracted me from being self-absorbed with my woes and gave me a more positive outlook and greater optimism. We benefit tremendously when we give to and do for others. It increases our blessings and grows us in innumerable and immeasurable ways.

When I was younger, having my baby sister to look after saved me from self-destructive behavior like joining a gang, committing suicide, or provoking someone else to end my life. Having the responsibility of caring for my first two wives and their children motivated me to achieve and gave me the inspiration I needed to make it home safely from dangerous assignments. As a corpsman charged with the lives and well-being of my Sailors and Marines, there was a never-ending supply of needs to meet, which always caused me to look beyond myself and any self-defeating thoughts I may have momentarily entertained.

Breaking unhealthy and ineffective cycles has been absolutely critical to my survival and thriving. Many of us are familiar with the definition of insanity, which is doing the same things and expecting different results. The challenge for me was that I was always so busy "doing", constantly in motion, which made it difficult, if not impossible, to see some of the behaviors and choices I was repeating. For a very long time, my indication that something needed to change was when I reached my mental and emotional limits of coping, or when it became clear that safety could be an imminent concern.

Leaving home at age eighteen was my first attempt at breaking an unhealthy cycle to pursue a more fulfilling and empowered existence. My decision to terminate my marriages and a few other significant relationships resembled my initial attempt, but something critical was still evading me as I was still making slightly different versions of the same choices and repeatedly finding myself in similar circumstances. How could I change something that escaped my awareness?

The journey to the development of the superpower of breaking cycles truly began when I spent that summer in the VA. It was here where I had no choice but to slam on the brakes and take a long, hard look at myself, my history, and all that led me where I had landed. The combination of a phenomenal staff, my curiosity, and my willingness to submit to the process started me on a trajectory of continuous learning, self-discovery, and self-improvement, all fueled by my intense desire to break every cycle that does not serve me.

Today, I am the President and majority owner of an Information Technology (IT) company that has solved many problems for the federal government and private industry for over thirty years. Absolutely every job, every military and educational experience I have had has led me here; the lessons and skills I gained along the way continue to serve me well, as I draw upon many of them daily. Faith in the Divine, unrelenting belief in myself and my abilities, charging forward in the face of adversity, and deep gratitude for all I have in every moment are also critical elements of my success.

By grace, my journey continues, and I now face each experience and challenge with eagerness and enthusiasm, ready for the next adventure! With all that I have endured, I celebrate that I am still here and growing in every way. This knowledge gives me peace and confidence that I have unlimited potential. What was once my ceiling has become my cellar, and the sky is only the beginning! Employing the tools that have served me well over the years and learning new methods from inspiring leaders who have also triumphed enhance my courage to brave the unknown. It allows me to be bold enough to face people and circumstances that may have once given me pause.

My story is still unfolding, and I am excited to see where the next chapter takes me. But one thing is certain: I will continue using my experiences, skills, and superpowers to positively impact and inspire others to overcome their challenges. Together, we can create a brighter future and improve the world.

While I may not possess superhuman abilities or wear a cape, I believe that each of us can be a hero in our own way. It is not the external circumstances that make us heroes, but rather, our choices and actions in the face of adversity. It is the willingness to step up, make a difference, and be a force for good in the world.

As I close, I want to acknowledge you, my cherished reader, for still being here despite any obstacles that could have prevented this. Whether your challenges involve family, poverty, mental health, self-doubt, relationships, abuse, or any combination of the above, I applaud you for hanging in. I celebrate your courage to move forward another day.

It has been an honor to be vulnerable with you in this publication, sharing some intimate moments in my journey that have brought about some of my most significant transformations and shaped the person I have become. For many of us, especially those who have served, vulnerability is a tricky word. However, I have learned to embrace the fact that if I want to be an effective leader, have authentic relationships, and experience true love, I must be okay with being a little vulnerable. If I successfully brought something positive to you with anything I have shared, it was worth it in every way.

Thank you for reading. Thank you for allowing me to be part of your world for a little while.

Superhero Life Lessons

By Robert W. Jones

Sometimes what you think you love the most turns out to be what you hate the most, and then as you grow and gain clarity, you find out that you loved it more than you ever would have thought. That seems like a strange paradox, when I look back at the clarity of my life, after these many years of both being a civilian and being in the military. As a kid, I idolized my Uncle Bob, who served in the Vietnam War, but as a community communications expert in the European theater. He was the guy who I wanted to be—someone who was a hero, someone who was looked up to, someone who beat the odds being from the inner city of Kansas City, KS, when no one thought that he had a chance.

He made something great out of his life and that's what I wanted to do—make something great out of my life. And like any young buck such as myself, when I was 12/13/14 years old, I thought, "Heck, he was in the army. Didn't know I was going to be in the Marines." And that's what I did. I started painting my world, a vision of being in the Marines. Taking up what I thought I knew of the world, making it mine, and letting everyone around me know who I was. Becoming a marine for me was the first time I ever could feel that I could breathe, and live, and had purpose. Prior to that for much of my life, I didn't have much purpose because I had to live in the shoes of both my dad and my mom.

Both my parents were extremely accomplished and actually did some world firsts in their careers—in academics, in business, and in their post-business careers. It really is funny, when I look back at who I was as a child, not feeling like I had a place to belong. I really was from two worlds—my dad was Caucasian, my mom was Mexican, and it seemed like I always landed somewhere in between when I tried to fit in. I had a tough time in school because I was also very shy, had a speech impediment, and was very awkward. It didn't take long for me to get past the awkwardness once I found out that I was actually a pretty great athlete. Once I started getting some confidence as an athlete, it started to affect other areas of my life.

And the greatest areas that it affected was that of doing something bigger than myself, being a champion for the underdog, and having a voice for others when they didn't have a voice for themselves. I remember the first time I went to the recruiter's office; it was the most exciting day of my life up to that point. It's like I could breathe in the history of the armed forces, and I could see myself in the place in that history, standing on a podium with ribbons, music blaring in the background and people saluting me, as I took another award for my outstanding duty and service. I was 17 years old when I joined, that was back in 1982. I hadn't even started my senior year quite yet, but every weekend, I was out there working out and becoming the best version of myself at the time.

I remember going through my senior year. It was kind of a blur, because as much as I wanted to embrace that last year of my education in high school, I still had these thoughts of what it was going to be like after I got out of high school; knowing that I was going to do something in life. I had worked at a restaurant as a dishwasher, a short order cook, a broiler, and a waiter and did many other things. I always was active, but at the end, it was just money. It wasn't really what I was looking for in my life. What I knew, was once I graduated high school, and with my outstanding ASVAB score, I was going to be able to do pretty much anything I wanted to do with my military career.

My number-one goal was to utilize my military career, because my aim was always to become a communications center officer. When I was signing up for my MOS (military occupational specialty), they didn't have room for me to be what I wanted to do, so I become a field radio communications operator and got to be with the infantry for much of my time. Although I had a great time in that service capacity, it really wasn't what I wanted to do. What I wanted to do was to be in communications; what I wanted to do was go to college; what I wanted to do was go to Officers Candidate School and change the world.

Unfortunately, all of that didn't happen for me. What did happen was I got to spend the first three years bounced back and forth between different companies, trying to utilize what talents I did have.

I still remember being deployed to Panama and being a naive 18year-old young adult, thinking that the world loved us, and finding out that, in fact, most of the world kind of loathed us. We were there on service duty when the when the Panama Canal was being turned back over to the Panamanians. I mean it was like bedlam every day. I mean I can still remember the smells of the food, the smell of the sweat, the smell of the trees and the Bush and the grass, and I remember how naked I was out there, toting a rifle with no ammunition. That was pretty much my first three years getting acquainted with what life was like in the military. There were no podiums for me to stand on; there was no saluting me from the stands; and there was no silver jet taking me to the White House to greet the President. What it really was was the sweet taste of the grind—of what it was to be the military enlisted officer.

When I signed up for my second three years, I was fortunate enough to get the MOS that I wanted. That was to be a call-center operator. I remember going out to Oceanside, living on base at Camp Pendleton, and learning the craft and skills that I really wanted. Then it happened; I found out that I didn't sign up with the GI bill and I was ******. I was ****** because I thought I was lied to. In fact, what I was was unaware. I wasn't aware that it was me that should have known to read the dotted lines on whether or not I was going to get that GI bill to pay for college. Nevertheless, I was ******, and that started the downward spiral of my desire to be in the military. Here I was thinking all my life that this is the "plus place" from which I would get my life, my career, my future family, and my retirement, and I was lied to.

I stood up and stood strong, and I still was a great marine. But I wasn't the marine that was gonna stand the test of time, and be in there 20, 25, or even 30 years, as a career Marine Corps member. My goal was to finish my next three years of duty and get out and move on with my life, never to look back, never to care about turning my back on some of the very people that I loved and I relied on when I served.

It wasn't until about 8 years ago, when I was about 50 years old, that I started softening in my feelings about my Marine Corps service. The first person who stepped into my life was Doctor Joe Blake, a career Air Force veteran, who served as a fireman. The first time I listened to him speak on what service meant to him, it made me reflect on my career and what I did or did not make of my career. He talked about service not being just the years that you take the government check, but service is all the years that follow, to take care of those who had served our government, our nation, and the people of our community that are all around us.

So here I am 50 years old, thinking to myself, "Man I have to grow up after all these years. I have to grow up. I need to be the person that I originally thought I would be, when I was 15 years old, some 35 years before." And as I started tracking on some of the people that also served with pride, and some who served with little bit of resentment, I started to compile a feeling that I wanted to be that guy who may have felt like he had been burned by the service, but I still wanted to be that guy that knew he was going to be of service to the very people who served—just like me. I wanted to be among the ones who may feel a little resentful, but when they really look back, they also had the greatest of relationships that they'll forever have in their lives, maybe other than the one that they have with God or their wife.

People often asked me, "What have you learned in this journey?" and I have to say there are many things that I've learned in this journey, and these are the things that I would like to share with you right now. The superhero tactics that I employ and that I learned from, not only my time in the six years that I served in the United States Marine Corps, but in the last six years plus, that I have served with the veterans who I now have around me, whom I know and love right now. These are SuperHero tactics that I employ every day in my international organization.

1. Life is perspective: if you haven't lived 4 lifetimes by the time you're 50, you don't have perspective.

2. People may be in a system, but people aren't the system. Know the difference between the two.

3. Success isn't lived on the outside. It is celebrated on the outside and lived on the inside.

4. When I was young, it was about winning, but as I have gotten older, I discovered that it is about succeeding.

5. Never close the door on a bad experience. Leave it open to learn its lesson.

Sharing the Pain

By Granny Lisa Kraft

It was just starting to rain in the forested area of Ft. Jackson, South Carolina when I heard the words, "You failed".

Walking past the long line of fellow soldiers waiting to pass their final Physical Test (PT), I held back the tears, thinking I will have to complete basic training again all because I couldn't do 13 men push-ups. I excelled at every task in boot camp and won special rewards for doing so. I shot expertly; I could hit targets with every weapon given to me. Yet, I could not do push-ups. Eighteen years old with a horrible past, and the military was my only hope of a bright future. What does a young woman do now? We will come back to this in a moment....

Raised in a small town of Oregon, I was termed "a lost cause". I had a handful of friends whom I cherished, and family was something I had but didn't want. Abuse and neglect lead to many decisions a child should never have to make, which left a now teen distraught with life, and wondering what was the meaning of even living. Pain and uncertainty were my constant companions, and most would say I was an angry teen with a chip on my shoulder. Defiant and outspoken, with no respect to adults, who either used me or abused me in one form or another. In all the mess of a child living through adult situations, I did learn about God. I so wanted Him to take me away, but it never happened. I believed He was real and wanted to believe He loved me, yet He was so distant, and so I just kept on reading His words in the Bible and tried the best I could on having blind faith. Faith, determination, give it my all or nothing attitude on one side, and fear, feeling not good enough, fearing to be always a failure, and feeling that I would always be white trash on the other side were the two conflicting voices within me. The battles and scars were deep inside the young heart of a warrior being developed. Some say we have defining moments in our lives that will knock you over. There is nothing else to explain it. Was this one on that day at Ft. Jackson—that defining moment?

With each step, my combat boots were losing their shine, as the rain now cascaded down onto the ground, forming puddles of mud. The pure silence of the walk of shame built more and more. The tears building yet not falling. As I kept passing soldiers waiting for their own fate that day. I'm passed the line and I hear a male voice with the authority of a seasoned Drill Sgt say, "Get back in line". I turned to look behind me expecting another Drill Sgt, and there was no one there. Turning back around, I heard the male voice with severe demands utter loudly, "I said get back in line now!" I knew when I turned around, no one would be there, I also knew in that instant I did not want to argue with that commanding voice and quickly got back into the line of doom. Nothing else was said, no particular feeling I had except I did learn to follow orders and this male voice wasn't messing around.

    A choice was made at that instant. Life would never be the same again. As each step drew me closer to the two Drill Sgts, the question came, "What am I going to do?" No answers came. Then the moment came, and I stood before the man who said I failed. He looked at me with such surprise and his eyebrows drew close in almost anger and said, "You failed, what do you want?" Without a hesitation, I got down into a now well-formed puddle of water, as the other (female) Drill Sgt next to him in her Dress Greens was looking at me with confusion as to what in the world I was doing. When my body gets into the push-up position, hands covered with mud and water, I say, "I want to prove to you that I can do my push-ups". By this time, a crowd had gathered around this young warrior's heart, and I started doing the best push-ups I could muster, shaking and still trying. I finally hear the words...1...2, with more failed ones in-between, the count of the push-ups kept getting bigger until I was done in. No more. I am at 10 and I can't keep from falling. I arch my back shaking and yell at the top of my lungs, "God, You said You would never leave me nor forsake me." Pure silence. The female Drill Sgt got into the mud puddle with me and started to yell out, "Do it, soldier," encouraging me to complete the task. I felt an enormous strength within my body as the Hand of God took hold and somehow pumped out three more push-ups. Jumping up after hearing 13, the male Drill Sgt changed the card and said, "If you tell anyone what has happened, I will deny it." He then gave all the other soldiers who failed their test another chance. That day was graduation day from Basic Training. I missed that ceremony. My best friend was an atheist, and before we parted ways, she told me she was going to pray to my God that I will pass my PT test. In blind faith I said, "God will answer your prayer." Upon returning to the barracks, it was complete chaos. I found her packed and ready for her next step of AIT. Quickly I told her of the accounts of what happened and she, in complete shock, said, "God is real then." No more doubts, and she quickly boarded the bus to start her life in the military.

    Today was an ordinary day. The long stone carved stairs up to the main street of Fish Alley wasn't a difficult climb. But it was difficult, since

The South Koreans stared at me in a soldier's uniform, being tall and not the normal picture they see. The busy sounds of the crazy traffic with the foreign languages surrounding me completely, I would hail down a Korean taxi and say, "Yongsan?" I would try to block the scene of the traffic and enjoy the views of my first time overseas, the excitement, and having my husband transferred with me made it so much more special. Our newest adventure added to our lives is the announcement that I was pregnant. I was on post in no time and arrived at my duty station. I began doing small chores around the office when the SSG came in and made his usual complaints about how women being in the military was wrong. I was 19 years old and did not dare say anything back to my superior. He would then leer at me like I was something below his boots. Then the other PFC soldier would enter, and the two men would start talking and cracking jokes about the Korean women and sexual things. I would tune them out and go about my duties, feeling uncomfortable but not sure what I could do about it. I would walk past the SSG, and he would slap my butt, making crude comments on how he should take that ass and own it. The two men would laugh and do some stuff. I left the main room, and when I returned, it was a completely different atmosphere.

    The two men are smiling at me when I go to the counter and start doing paperwork. I feel a presence behind me. I turn to look around and the SSG hand pushes my head swiftly and hard onto the counter. His breathing is now on my neck leaning into my body pressing it harder into the counter. The smell of His Old Spice cologne seems to be choking my throat and burning my nose. He says happily and loudly, "I'm going to show you why a female should never join the military." With his hands on my shoulders, he pulls me back against him as he begins to assault my breasts, while the other soldier is watching, and they say comments back and forth. His hands seem to be everywhere at once as he assaults me from behind. I zoned out. All I did was notice the handles on the drawers across the counter. The bite he gives my neck brings me out of my trance when I feel his body leave, and the other soldier comes to replace him. The handles on the drawers were brass, not very ornate, just dingy brass handles. I've seen much prettier ones on drawers.

    He was younger and not experienced in rape, so it was over with rather quickly. Then, everything went right back to normal. Nothing horrible just happened. They were at their desks working away. I straightened myself up, went to the bathroom and stared into the mirror in shock. Did this really happen? Did I just allow two men to do this to me and didn't even fight back? What the hell is wrong with me? What do I do now? I go home like nothing happened. I just continue on for another two weeks of harassment, of snide remarks, of touching and slapping my butt or fondling my breasts when I try to walk past quickly. I had enough. When my husband would come and visit at my work, they all three were buddies while I worked, and the SSG would brag about how great of a worker I was. I eventually told my husband that I was being harassed at work. I didn't say what happened. I couldn't tell him. Since I didn't make a huge deal, he suggested I go to my chain of command.

The very next day I went to the chain of command and told him what was happening and what had happened. He said in a matter-of-fact tone that he would take care of it. I was so naive for believing that statement. Days passed when it continued, and then the day of anger appeared into the office and yelling how dare I tell lies about him assaulting me and touching me inappropriately. He said that I was a bitch and this is why females shouldn't be in the military. I was terrified. My heart was racing; there was no escape. There was never going to be any relief from this torture of never knowing what or when something would happen to me. He came right up to my face, leaned in, and yelled, while I felt the wind from his mouth and smelled his breath, "You ever say anything again about me, you will live to regret it. You got that?" All I could do was nod my head and run from the office.

I don't know how far I went running, trying not to cry, just wanting to be home and not here where I was trapped. I stopped to see where I was on the post and gather my senses. I was standing in front of the JAG Office. I go inside and ask to see someone to help me with a problem. I see an officer; he sits me down, and I share the story from beginning to this end where I ended up at his office. He is took notes and asked a few questions and looked at me with all seriousness, "I will get back with you on this. Just continue doing your job." I left with a pit in the bottom of my stomach. What did I just do? This isn't going to be good.

The next day I started up those same cut stone steps to the top of the street of the neighborhood where I lived off base. The little old man, who was always set up with a paper stand at the top, smiled and did his usual greeting. I did the fake smile and hailed a taxi to go to the place of torture and no escape. You just can't quit the Army; you can't just not show up. There are severe punishments for that kind of thing. Yet, assaulting a female soldier isn't something taken seriously? How does this make sense? It doesn't, so I just tried to pretend like nothing happened and did my job.

Once I went to the office, I was told to report to the commander immediately. My stomach dropped, here it comes, I'm in trouble. I did the proper procedure of greeting and was told to sit down. First words. "I told you I would handle this, and you go to JAG and report the SSG who is a decorated Vietnam soldier ready to retire. Do you realize that this will destroy his career and his retirement? His family who depend on him is now lost, because you say he assaulted you, and a new PFC who isn't even 21, his life will be tarnished forever." I was in shock again; complete confusion, and I am feeling guilty. He continues with his next barrage of assault, "This is what I will do. I won't cause you to be charged or lose rank. I know you are pregnant and so this obviously is a violent situation. I will move you to a better work environment; you drop the charges and everyone will be happy, and there will not be anyone losing anything in the ordeal." I'm shaking with fear, and this 19-year-old girl is railroaded into compliance and agrees and even says she is sorry for causing so much trouble.

I did drop charges and was moved to a whole different area where I would never see that SSG again. What did I do with all this trauma and the reason I acted the way I did? What was even more crazy is that I never once mentioned the incident to my husband. Never once. It was only this year 2023, now divorced, and he never understood what happened to his wife, who was once fun, loving, strong, didn't take crap even from him, spiraling out of control. That woman he fell in love with disappeared, and some stranger was now there. So many problems afterwards, and no one talked about depression or trauma then.

Plus, when you don't share what the trauma is, it only compounds everything. Once we talked and I told him what happened, he didn't believe me at first because I always acted just fine when he came to visit the office. All of us were joking and talking and things were great. Then the picture began to come clear to him and boom, "Why didn't you tell me? I would have protected you. Things would have been so different." I only replied, "I know it's not your fault; I didn't tell you." The real reason I didn't say anything is that I had subconsciously buried a troubled childhood of sexual assault. I was groomed to respond the way I did when put into a similar situation. Not even my brain remembered, but the body never forgets. It wasn't until in my late 30s that those memories came haunting me, and it's been something I now deal with, plus the MST. Sometimes, smelling the cologne Old Spice sends me right back to the scene in front of me. The hauntings happen while I am sleeping, cleaning, driving, and when it happens in public places, I try to escape quickly. I'm ready to defend myself from any man who dares to approach me at this time of panic. My body feels everything, fresh pain, chest hurts, buttocks burn, intimate places hurt from the abuse of being violated. I try to concentrate on my breathing, doing the tapping method, slowly blowing my breaths out; trying to avoid the real actions I want to do.

The worst decision I ever made in my life was dropping those charges and not sharing what happened to my husband at the time. My life fell downward quickly. I became severely depressed. I didn't care about myself, and so I gained weight. I became more lost and confused. I ended up a divorced, single mom, even more depressed without knowing why. In those times, PTSD or mental illness were not commonly spoken about. It wasn't until I was hospitalized and tried to get a disability rating that I was quickly denied because my records of the time had disappeared. I just stayed in the system of mental illness, in and out, going from job to job, not understanding why I couldn't get my act together. Every time I started to succeed, I would fall flat on my face. No self-confidence, and to be honest, I didn't have any support system from my family. It was easier for them to continue the cycle of cutting me down and basically saying I was a loser. You know it was easier for them to say, "Hey, at least I'm not as bad as Lisa is!" It made them feel better in some horrendous way. Yet again they had a lot to hide, keeping their demons from the public.

Forty plus years later, I have finally gotten my disability rating. Am I still in therapy? Yes, I am. In the years trying to forget it, I did more damage by trying to bury it. What is the reason I am sharing this with you? Well, first off, I didn't do anything wrong to be assaulted. A lifetime was stolen from me because I kept quiet and hid it. I did share the same story consistently in my counseling for years in the VA system, and I endured so many drugs that I am wondering how I can even think straight now. Although my family probably has a different opinion on that. (humor)

I want to share that there is help; that being quiet isn't the way to handle sexual abuse, rape, harassment, touching, threats, and/or poking fun at your body parts. This is not OK, and the women who encourage this kind of behavior are part of this problem too. Using your sex appeal to move forward or gain special treatment is part of the problem of why it continues to this day. When the line is crossed, there is most likely no one in the immediate command who's going to be there for you. That is a truth; you may have an officer who is sympathetic to your situation. Yet, all he is thinking is how to get rid of this problem without the higher ups finding out. No officer wants this kind of stain on his/her command. Don't think that, if it's a female officer, that it will be different. There is hope; you need to go to the doctor and request seeing a counselor. Gather your evidence of times and places you need to keep records of the events because you will forget those details. Keep them safe and not on your phone but in written form locked up in a bank or sent to a family member. Keep video logs and forward them to someone you trust. However you do it, you need to keep yourself safe and protected until the issues are resolved. Request all your military records during that time period so you can make sure there is nothing missing from your files.

I can say that I am in a better place in my life after getting and continuing to get the help I need. It has also given me security that I have not had since leaving the military, in having my rating. I am no longer a victim. I am an advocate for dealing with MST. It is important that veterans are there for each other. For no one understands a vet like another vet. So… don't give up, don't give in. Fight and speak loudly. Walk proudly and make your words count for something.

In all this craziness, I do miss the structure of the military. I knew what my job was. I knew what was expected in all aspects of my time in the military. I enjoyed meeting different people from different places, of different races, and with different languages spoken. There are wonderful people in the military—comrades I will never forget. They ask what are your superpowers, Lisa? What wisdom do you want to impart to other veterans so they are not left behind?

I don't believe I have any superpowers; I think I have what anyone else has who has been in the military or in the military right now. If you want to think of them as superpowers, then that's great. I believe that I am a Warrior! I fight for what I believe; I may be in the fight for a long time. Yet I am a Warrior!! We have Pride in what we do. We take each moment and look to our left and right and never leave another behind. We are Warriors who Pride ourselves in our job, working together or alone, it all goes towards the goal. We may not like the person next to us, yet Lord have mercy on your soul if you try to take that person out of the picture. We have Loyalty! So, I am Loyal, and I find it difficult to understand how it doesn't always work. These are just three superpowers I have touched on. We know there are so many more superpowers. We possess endurance, physical strength/pain, quick decisions under mental fatigue, run towards death, leave no soldier behind; we possess humor, passion, love, sense of duty, love for our freedoms, love for our families.

You are a hero in the service of the United States Military, period. Combat, non-combat, behind a desk, or wherever you were.

I do a podcast called "Vets Chatting with Granny Lisa". I interview veterans who share their organizations or stories of military life and afterwards. My email is: grannylisastudio12@gmail.com God bless you, Soldier and Veteran! You have my deepest respect, and I stand next to you today in the best way I can, to support you and encourage you. No matter what you have experienced, what choices you have made, what things that happened to you. You are a Soldier and/or Veteran!!! We have you. Did you hear me? We got you! Just let us know how we can help. Veterans are ready to help veterans...We don't leave a soldier behind.

      With Granny's Hugs—and I mean the hugs that you can rest your head up against and feel the warmth of all the way to your toes. A soft voice saying, "I love you; You're going to be alright." Reach out and talk to me,

Granny Lisa

You Are Worthy

By Michiel "All Mike" Montiel

Name: Gary Michiel Montiel
Codename: "All Mike"
Place of Origin: Sonoran Desert
City: Superior, Arizona
Age: 40 years old
Special abilities: Haphazard courage, radical empathy, and stalwart perseverance

Abstract:

Subject is known throughout his community as a warrior and a leader within his areas of expertise, this includes: combat operations, leadership, and community development. 'All Mike' serves as team member, comrade, supporter, ally, and commander in service of his family, his country, and his people. He was raised by the unforgiving desert landscape that formed him to be as stout and tough as a barrel cactus. His youth was spent isolated from much of society, which led him to be considered a loner or outsider, even within his own tribe and family. During his military career he was faced with death, destruction, and mayhem. None of these adversities dissuaded him from entering the fray of combat at a moment's notice. After his military career, he was under siege by his own destructive behaviors, habits, and mindset. These setbacks only served to harden his already thick skin, but surprisingly, also led him to open his heart to others he saw struggling. He now recruits others to find their purpose, by inspiring them to be their authentic selves and be courageous. Subject should be considered a catalyst for change and a major threat to any organization or structure that seeks to harm, injure, disenfranchise, or destroy.

Autobiography:

Most great stories about heroes begin with a young person who is unsure of their place in this world and of how their presence might be felt. They play the part of the "reluctant hero". Our lives come with a multitude of trials and tribulations for survival alone, but being forced to learn to thrive in difficult, stressful, or even abusive environments can hinder or delay the progression of people, regardless of age, sex, background, or personality. To become a leader worthy of the moniker "hero", one must overcome not only the journey we choose for ourselves, but also the odyssey life chooses for us. My story unfolds relatively the same in this way, with my very own crucibles of fire, loss, and redemption.

The early years…

I was born to a single mother, who, only weeks before my emergence into this world, left my abusive father, because she feared for our family's safety. I recall overhearing the stories about how my mother lost multiple children while pregnant due to my father's physical abuse, and that both my sister and my births were nothing short of "miraculous". In fact, immediately after I made my way onto this floating blue sphere we call Earth, my mom had to undergo emergency hysterectomy surgery because of the issues during my gestation and birth. Due to complications from birth and surgery, I did not feel the warmth of my mother's embrace until I was 5 days old; I do not recall meeting my father until I was 11 years old. Both of these facts had significant effects on me back when I was just a young boy and even as a grown man.

From a very young age, I found hesitation meant certain defeat, regardless of the adversary. I can remember vividly the last time I hesitated or tried to run from a fight; I was in the 7th grade and I had a bully, who was 3 years older than I and in high school. The bully was much larger and stronger than I was at the time, but there was something inside of me that never let me back down. The beginning of our rivalry was him attempting to verbally belittle me, like he did everyone else that rode our bus. He had a stocky build, sported a long dirty blonde mullet, and dressed in the style of bikers, with a long wallet chain, boots, and rough attitude included.

I remember the day our heated verbal exchange escalated to violence. On the morning ride to school, in our rural mining town in the eastern Arizona mountains, we began the ride with him doing as he did most days—going around harassing the girls whom he liked and physically intimidating any boys who dared look his way. That particular day, I had enough of his attempts to start picking at me, so I told him in no uncertain terms exactly where to go. I did this loudly and clearly in front of everyone on the bus, all of whom met my words with a roar of cheers, laughter, and "Oooohs". As you may recall, the long "Oooohs" are usually followed by fighting words. My bully took this as his opportunity to finally feel justified in commencing the beat-down he had always wanted to give me.

Since I was still in junior high and he was in high school, the stops we got off the bus were different, so he would have to wait until the end of the day to thrash me. He said very clearly, "I am gonna beat your a** after school! And no one can save you!" I could see in his eyes that his words were not empty but filled with angst and rage. It was at this moment the sinking feeling of dread began to creep into my stomach. My heart began to race, and my mind became caught in a cycle of fear and worry. What was a 12-year-old pre-pubescent kid doing going up against a 15-year-old young man? The guy had at least 20 pounds, 4 inches, and a whole lot of testosterone in his corner. I had been in numerous fights with kids around my age, but even the heavies I had fought in the past were nothing compared to this monster of a young man, who wanted nothing more than to rip me to shreds.

    I got off the bus already dreading the bell at 3:30pm, because on that day, it would not only toll for the end of the day at school but would toll the pain I was going to feel at the hands of my bully. The day was like every other day, other than the increasing cloud of terror that grew over me—a reality that was only made worse by the fact that some of my fellow bus riders went around telling everyone else there was going to be a fight. I spent half the day trying to calculate a plan of escape. I went to the nurse's office and played sick; they gave me some Motrin then called my mom. But I would not receive a reprieve from what was coming that day.

    After the final bell of the day tolled, I began my slow trudge toward the violence that awaited me. Junior highers, high schoolers, and grade schoolers loaded the buses at the same spot so I knew there would be no avoiding him. But I thought maybe, if I walked slowly enough, I could stall my death sentence long enough to avoid the encounter entirely. I had no idea that, after not seeing me at the bus stop, that he would begin walking down the hill toward my classroom to find me.

    I clearly recall the jolt of absolute horror I felt when I looked up from my "trail of terror" and saw him coming towards me with the expression of absolute hate in his eyes, and the look of glee plastered all over his face at the prospect of punching my face in. I don't even think I had the time to formulate words to say to him before he was upon me. His fevered footsteps were followed by the throwing of well-practiced jabs and haymakers intended to knock my head clean off. One of his jabs landed squarely on my nose; that was when I could begin to feel the gush of warm blood erupting from my face. I tried to throw a few meager punches at his head, but his height and reach advantage made it almost impossible. Then he threw a haymaker that connected with my jaw, I immediately felt my teeth grind together, spurting blood on the inside of my mouth mixing, with the flavor of ground chunks of tooth inside, then dripping down my throat. I decided to finally make a lunge at him hoping to take him down, maybe get a punch or two in and save myself from such a terrible defeat. I pushed forward with all my might and managed to grab him around the waist and use my low center of gravity to take him to the ground. That would be the only measurable success I had in our fight. Once we were on the ground, he used his insurmountable weight advantage to pin me down and straddle above me, from where he just started wailing away at my face. I did my best to keep my hands up and protect myself. I recall the slapping noise his fists made against the backs of my hands and forearms as he tried to pummel me into the pavement. Then, finally help arrived in the form of a high schooler named Peter who saw this huge teenager mounted on top of me and took pity on me.

My savior that day pushed the bully off me and told him to, "Cut it the hell out; that's just kid!" The bully immediately realized he was vastly outgunned, as Peter was a varsity football player and was not to be trifled with. The bully walked away with a huge smile on his face as though he had just accomplished something great by beating me up. Peter helped me to my feet, and the only words I remember him saying to me were, "Damn kid! You're tough! That dude was way bigger than you!" I still remember the feelings of pain I felt in my body; the bloody nose, the sore jaw, the road rash I had all over my arms from wrestling on the ground. To my surprise, I could see the looks of the other kids that watched the fight, it was not looks of sympathy but admiration and shock. The air reeked of genuine surprise that this kid not only stood up to this bully, but he stood relatively unscathed and now unafraid.

That a** whooping I took was a defining moment for me as a boy. I learned that safety was not something we can negotiate, run to, or be provided by others. I learned that instead of seeking safety, I should seek the ability to stand up for myself, regardless of the situation in which I find myself. I found my "Haphazard Courage".

This combination of words may be misleading to some, so let me better define the term. Haphazard courage is the willingness to throw caution to the wind and run headlong into the crucible of conflict. It is not the belief you can win every battle, but instead, that you can change one thing in the fight. Sometimes that means a single take-down; sometimes it just means not backing down in the face of certain defeat. I will always do at least one thing, no matter the odds stacked against me.

One thing I am very certain of about myself is that I am human, I was born of my mother and my father. I am not perfect by any measure of the word, and that means I will make mistakes; I will miscalculate and underestimate things, and I will most assuredly fall short of the glory. However, this does not mean that I should shy away from conflict or hardship, but rather that my willingness to face them will place me in the best position to have a shot at being victorious and snatching that which is mine from the jaws of defeat. In my humble opinion, there is no higher courage one can show than honest self-reflection in which a person sits with their faults, mistakes, and shortcomings, but does not become overly engrossed in them so that they become a hindrance to growth and development. In fact, it is when we fail that we will learn the most important lessons about life and face the genuine measure of our abilities in the face of adversaries and challenges.

Take the leaps which call to your heart. If you have a vision, work towards it with the passion and resources you have; do not wait. If you hear a calling, heed the words you hear in your mind; do not doubt yourself. If you feel drawn to something, follow the path; do not hesitate. Your greatness and your destiny are waiting on the other side of the bloody noses, pain, and discomfort you will feel. Move forward headlong towards your vision, your calling, and the things you are drawn to, and the world will stand in awe of all of your accomplishments, no matter what.

As a young man...

I have known I wanted to be a soldier for as long as I can remember—when I was very young, that was mainly because I loved G.I. Joes, green army men, and crawling around in the wilderness, turning every stick into a rifle and every pinecone into a grenade. This desire was cemented when I was a young man during a car ride with my mother.

I grew up knowing several of my uncles had fought for our country during the Korean War and Vietnam conflict, but none of them ever spoke much about their service. And I had very little knowledge, as the history lessons would not come until later in my education during college. During that fateful car ride with my mother, we were on a monthly supply run down to the "Valley", also known as Phoenix, when the Lee Greenwood song "Proud to be an American" came on the radio, and I saw my mother, who was a very tough and solemn woman, begin to cry. Very concerned, I asked her, "Momma, what's wrong?" At that point she began to explain to me the sacrifices my uncle Roy, her brother, made for our country during his time in Vietnam, as well as the pain he felt when he returned to an ungrateful nation during a very tumultuous time in our nation's history. As I listened and watched her carefully, the tears she shed were not ones of pain or anguish, but rather those of admiration and respect. It was in that moment of time that I knew the class of person I wanted to be; I wanted to be inducted into the warrior-class. I knew then I wanted to be the type of man who was looked at with respect for his sacrifice, courage, and willingness to bear the brunt of conflict.

My uncle Roy passed away several years ago due to complications from Agent Orange, and he is still sorely missed by my mother's family. My Tio (uncle) Bernie passed away several years ago, also due to complications from Agent Orange and is sorely missed by my father's family. My Uncle Jim and Uncle Bob both served and are still with us. These men provided the heritage and inspiration for my service, and I would not be the man I am without their examples.

It is because of the brave family members I have had as examples that I enlisted in the Army while still a junior in high school. It was during my time in uniform that I developed the most important leadership skill I have at my disposal, and that is "Radical Empathy". I define "Radical Empathy" as the ability to understand and acknowledge the feelings of others independent of your own attachments or intentions surrounding the situation. This does not require you to feel exactly what the person is experiencing, but rather, to make the other person feel validated that their emotional response is normal, and then, using that commonality, to frame the situation in a productive and/or healthy way. Radical Empathy also does not require you to understand why the person is reacting the way that they are – merely to observe and communicate in a healthy manner to improve the scenario, relationship, or situation.

This special ability was difficult to master because it forced me to care for others more than I cared for myself. Suspending your desire to operate solely in survival mode can be extremely difficult if you had an upbringing in which others did not try to address your basic needs of safety and security. It requires a person who is trying to display radical empathy to others to suspend their own thoughts, feelings, and preconceptions about a situation and instead engage with an open mind, devoid of judgments. While in the military, I never made the rank of a non-commissioned officer, but often operated in the capacity of one while performing the duties of a team leader for my squad. However, the little traditional training I had as an official leader of my peers, the practical application and practice leading others in garrison, on training missions, and in combat zones more than made up for any shortcomings.

As a leader, in the beginning, I would often just expect those lower in rank to be able to easily follow in my footsteps, especially when I taught them all the steps: studying, mentoring, practice, training, support, and accountability. But then one day I finally realized my fellow soldiers did not have the same advantages I did, and because of that, would not be able to follow my footsteps, because their feet were different sizes, their strides were different lengths, some were pigeon-toed, and some had flat feet.

There was one soldier in particular that solidified my higher aptitude for empathizing with others, but it was not to be an enjoyable experience. He came to our unit as a wet-behind-the-ears Private First Class, also known as a "PFC". And for the sake of the story, we will call him PFC Aubry, I use this pseudonym because I also wouldn't want to hurt his reputation back home due to the ridiculous nature of the tale I am about to tell.

At this time in my military career, I had given up on a campaign to go for the promotion to gain the rank of Sergeant. I had requested several times to be sent to soldier-of-the-month boards, which is a monthly competition within a battalion of around 1,000 soldiers. It tests general knowledge about military codes and rules of conduct but also job-specific knowledge of equipment specifications and all relevant crew drills. I never got to go, and to this day, I regret not advocating harder to be given the chance to prove myself in that way to myself, to my peers, and to my leaders.

When PFC Aubry first arrived, I was happy to welcome a new soldier to our artillery gun section... a new soldier meant less work for me.
And I was a proud member of the 'E4 Mafia'.
*** **Historical context:**
E4 Mafia—The name has no organizational meaning and is not an entity as the moniker implies. It is in fact, just a bunch of men and women from all around the United States armed forces that make it to the rank of E4 but for whatever reason, do not move forward in their ascension of the military ranks, *i.e.* Sergeant. These individuals have spent so much time mastering their craft that they have been assigned that they do it to the highest level of professionalism and proficiency. So much so, that they can achieve their mission in a very short amount of time compared with peers. They are highly capable individuals who, if properly managed, can be one of the most powerful tools a leader has at their disposal.
Note—Officers and high-ranking non-commissioned officers cannot stand to see enlisted men and women not spending every waking minute of their duty hours doing something productive, by military standards. This includes cutting the grass with scissors, sweeping a dirt lot, hosing off a driveway while it is raining, mowing synthetic grass, or holding a random tool like a broom or a shovel and just standing around. Clipboards are also acceptable accessories for looking productive when not really doing anything. ***

My time with PFC Aubry was, though I did not know it at the time, to be one of the most trying and educational times in my life, because it was a learned experience where I had to go through the nonsense to get to the lesson on the other side. For the most part, it was not a fun or enjoyable time for me or my direct leadership.

When young, red-haired, freckle-faced, 120-pound-soaking-wet PFC Aubry arrived, he seemed like he would be an easy FNG to work into the team.
*** **Definition: FNG- Acronym; F***ing New Guy.** The newest and lowest ranking member of a military squad, section, or line. They are required to do all the unwanted duties and perform most of the physical labor. ***

I liked him at first, because he said he loved his country and wanted to serve like his family did before him. That resonated with me. His special ability was physical fitness because of his light frame and high muscle content. Because of basic training, he could run like the wind and do push-ups/sit-ups like few other people I have ever seen. That is a huge plus for an FNG, because that is half of how the military gauges your combat readiness.

Shortly after coming to Charlie Battery Cobra's 3rd Platoon, PFC Aubry began displaying signs of strange behavior and total personal unawareness. I now know he was just incapable of understanding some concepts without rigorous structure and constant monitoring of the completion of responsibilities and tasks.

There are many stories of failure, embarrassment, and a** chewings because of the actions of this young man and his presence in my life. Some are just so ridiculous I would hesitate to tell them, and others so funny that I burst out laughing every time I tell them. I will share one story about an experience during this time; it overall is comedic but was also the moment I realized I had a special gift to try to share with others.

After about two months in my gun section, the crack around the edges of this kid did not just begin to show to those of us around him, but was clearly on display for all to see! He lacked any basic knowledge a soldier coming out of advanced individual training should have. He couldn't name the parts of the artillery piece he had trained on. But his physical fitness was still top notch. I tried to relate to him on a personal level, but we did not have much to connect about, other than his desire to make his family proud. Then one of the most ridiculous sequences of events began to unfold.

One afternoon just before end-of-day formation to be released for the day, everyone was informed that the platoon sergeants are going to do a health and welfare check of all the soldiers' rooms in the barracks, and that soldiers need to stand by their rooms. What they found in that young fool's room would go down in infamy.

Our entire section was called over to PFC Aubry's room almost immediately after it was inspected. The room was filth incarnate. Trash all over the floor. The bed was half made, and the sheets were stained. The room had a foul stench of stale sugar and sour laundry. *Le coup de gras*? The craziest part?? Why am I building suspense???

In the span of two months that grown little boy had drunk well over 900 cans of Mountain Dew sodas and piled them up very neatly on two tables to make a large rectangular, and I am quoting PFC Aubry here, a "Mountain of Dooooo". No one was amused at the 12-can-wide by 12-can-long by 6can-high spectacle (or monument!) to the unabashed nature of some people and how they live their lives.
*** **Math and Biology Note:** If a person accrues a stockpile of over 900 cans of Mountain Dew over a 2-month period, conservative estimation of their soda intake sits at around a 12-pack of sodas per day. USDA states at **4 sodas per day**, a person significantly increases their chance of obesity, heart disease, and diabetes. ***

Our Platoon Sergeant was very clear in his instructions, "No one is going anywhere until that boy's room is spotless. SPOTLESS!"

My section chief put PFC Aubry at parade rest with all of us in the room. He then proceeded to chew this kid a new a**hole. The kid was already skinny but by the time he was done with him the poor thing had no back side left. He called him all the variations of dirty and disgusting one could conjure in their mind. He spent about 5 minutes shredding a new orifice in the side of this young man's face. Then our Chief gave him the chance to speak. That's when I felt it. I felt the sensation of a deep and profound moment of enlightenment.

This young man who was educated at public school, graduated basic training, and completed his advanced individual training could not comprehend what he did wrong. He expected his leadership to come by and tell him all the little things he was doing wrong and how to fix them. He expected us to walk him through his everyday existence as a member of our gun section. He expected others to be more accountable for him than he was for himself. He was devoid of the ability to manage or regulate his compulsions—not to make short-sighted decisions, and not to behave like he was still an actual child once his uniform came off.

Once I took a moment to truly digest this new information about how to best lead PFC Aubry, a cascade of thoughts and emotions, relevant to leading others, began to align in my mind. I already understood the concepts of positive and negative reinforcement, but understanding what each individual person considers to be positive and negative is where the most valuable information lies. I never got the opportunity to thank that young man for the lesson, but I do not think he could conceptualize what I had come to internalize as such a huge lesson in my life. So, given the opportunity I would just tell him, "Thank you for being my soldier and holding the line."

Shortly after this incident, PFC Aubry would no longer be my responsibility or one of the troops I was responsible for because he developed diabetes. I have no doubt his predilection for the "Mountain of Doooo" sealed his fate. He was medically discharged from our ranks and never heard from again.

In the face of angry antagonists, inept leaders, and incapable team members, I retain my ability to ask the disarming questions which are able to create situations and relationships based in the truth and perception of others, instead of my own. I do not dismiss or devalue my own, but instead, capitalize on my ability to simultaneously hold my values and standards up as examples while getting others to invest themselves in the shared values and vision we have.

Lead others by being your authentic self. There is no one else in the world like you… Now start acting like it.

Post military life…

During my time in uniform, I developed an extremely high reputation and feeling of self-worth. At the time, I had no idea how intertwined my self-esteem was with my status as an active-duty soldier. I had no idea that when I separated from the army, that my feeling of value and worth would spiral down, leaving me an almost unrecognizable version of myself. I would not stay down forever, nor would my path to redemption be a straight one. The curves and contours of the road I traversed would be filled with difficulties, hardships, heartbreaks, indecision, frustration, and regrets. Some of these were self-inflicted, while others were things I could not even seen coming.

When I first returned to Arizona from my 4 years in the Army, I hit the ground running and kept up the break-neck speed that I had become accustomed to while in uniform. I enrolled at Mesa Community College and was taking 18 credit hours worth of classes in a single semester, which is a semester and a half worth of classes. I had a full-time job as shift manager for a retail shop and worked 40 hours a week. I kept this up for about a year before I hit a wall. Not literally, but a figurative wall, where I had to take a big step back from my life to reassess how I was living and get my mental health back on track. I believed myself so strong and capable that I didn't need any help, just a break. So, I took one.

During this time, I had to begin wrestling a number of the demons that I still engage with on a daily basis to this very day. Self- doubt, regret, anguish, impostor syndrome, survivor's guilt, and anxiety—all became regular featured characters in my mind. This had the effect of dampening my outlook on life and causing me to lose faith in myself. They would chip away at the essence of who I was. I did put up an admirable defense, clawing back pieces of myself, but without professional help, it was to be a doomed effort.

After taking a semester off from Mesa Community College, I re-enrolled and got back into the swing of things, but this time only taking the standard 12 credit hours of classes, and I began working for my cousin cleaning backyard pools in my area. I thought I had fought off the beasts at my door and was now eternally victorious. Boy was I wrong!

I began to have considerable struggles around social anxiety, specifically with large crowds and masses of people. I now know this was a response to the two years I served as an infantryman and deployed on a combat mission to Bayji, Iraq. While in country every man, woman, and child had to be considered a threat and be treated accordingly. We trained to fight insurgents, but even that is a difficult task, because how do you teach someone to discern threats in the midst of a bustling city, crowded highway, or sleepy village? It is almost impossible to adequately prepare for this kind of mission. The idea that the enemy is all around you really sinks in after you are attacked the third or fourth time, and causes you to take the stance of someone who can never relax or become complacent in watching your sector and making sure you got your battle buddies' '6'.
*****Verbal context:** The term "I got your 6" means to watch the rear of a fellow service member. This term has an element of overall safeguarding of fellow comrades. It has relevance in all aspects of military life. But, it has specific meaning in the combat arms units of the military where it means watching everyone's back so everyone can come home with their life and all 10 fingers and toes.***

While in Iraq, places and things that were previously mundane became sources of earth-shattering destruction and death. The world could shift at a moment's notice, and we always had to be ready for a fight. Improvised explosive devices, also known as IEDs or roadside bombs, were commonplace for my platoon while in Iraq. In fact, we became known as the IED Platoon because we were hit so often by these gargantuan stockpiles of artillery munitions wired to try to blow us up as we drove by. By some act of God or Providence, we never lost a soldier's life to one of these heinous creations set by insurgents to take us out. I still ruminate and pray on this fact to this very day. Mainly I feel gratitude but there is still an ominous feeling of deep-seated terror because I have seen what these machinations of pure destruction are capable of, and I do not know how I mentally or spiritually would have coped if I had had to witness the men I love to this day and call my brothers, fall victim to the total annihilation of a blast.

College campuses are filled with energy and life; they are bustling communities with unique cultures and architecture. One could even say each campus is its very own little city, because of the staff and infrastructure involved. Each school being located here in the States, consisting of multi-ethnic backgrounds, the modern feel of the space, and laid-back approach of most of its citizens SHOULD NOT elicit a fight-or flight response. But it did. And similar settings often still do. I felt instinctively compelled to remain vigilant at all times; I had to watch my sector; I had to keep an eye on all doors and windows; I had to assess every possible threat that crossed my path... It was and still is an exhausting undertaking, where, even if I enjoy the activity which brings me to a space with a large group, I cannot fully feel immersed or engaged, because that switch in my mind is still set to 'ON'.

I managed to muddle my way through and earned my associate's degree from Mesa Community College. My mother's lifelong lesson of education was still very strong in my mind, so I went on ahead and began my studies at Arizona State University. Now for those of you who are not familiar with ASU, it is a huge campus surrounded by a huge metropolitan area. The daily population of the main campus, where I attended, clocked in at around 50,000 people while I went to school there. For a small-town boy, this was surreal. Having spent some time as a younger man in the Phoenix metro area, I never imagined how many people you could pack into a very small geographical area of this city that I thought I knew, from the hours of 8am to 4pm every single day. But as always, it was my duty to soldier through.

And soldier through I did! I pushed past the feeling of anxiety, depression, and exhaustion to make it to being within 18 credits of graduating from ASU with my Bachelor's Degree—a feat only a handful of my family had ever undertaken, let alone achieved. Alas, I hit a wall again. Let me rephrase, I hit a f***ing mountain. The symptoms of PTSD had long been in the back of my mind because the VA counselors told one I had it, but it is one thing to hear someone say that, and an entirely different thing to internalize as fact. I had tried to convince myself that my symptoms were merely short-term things that, if I could just push past in that moment, then I would be fine. But I wasn't fine; I was not okay. This was the time when I

began to plot the end of my life.

It did not take me long to formulate the plan for my suicide. I lived by the gun, so I would die by the gun as well. I purchased a military style rifle, similar to the one I carried in Iraq, from a local pawn shop. It was brand new and in the box. My plan was that the only round to ever be fired from that weapon was going to be the one that ended my life. I bought a single box of 50 rounds of the highest quality ammo they had. The plan was set. But every day I considered springing the plan to action, there was a voice in my head that said, "Not yet." I can tell you for certain it was not the sound of my voice. I know how crazy that may sound, but I have small conversations with myself in my head often when contemplating or problem-solving, so I am very familiar with the tone and voice in my head. The voice I heard was something else entirely.

Friends who are spiritual have told me it was the voice of God telling me to stay a little while longer. Friends who are more scientific told me it was the reptile part of my brain seeking self-preservation. Part of me used to believe it was the cowardly part of my brain that was too scared to pull the trigger. These days, I don't know what to believe, other than that some sense I had within myself could feel that what I had to give the world was still within me, and creating an emotional reaction from my friends and family by taking my own life was not how I was going to share it. I had to persevere.

I re-entered counseling at the VA and began a long and arduous journey back towards a life I could be proud of. You see, at this point in my story, other than dropping out of college completely and becoming suicidal, I had also lost almost everything and became hopeless and homeless. Apathy and lack of joy were central themes during this time of my life. I wish I could say I was past them entirely, but I am not. I still struggle to remain motivated and engaged. It is often exhausting to be present in social settings. It can still be extremely uncomfortable for me to emotionally connect with others. As difficult as this era was for me, it was necessary for me to experience to realize I had to be proactive in my process of healing and transforming myself into the person I wanted to be.

Along with counseling, I also began volunteering with veterans' service organizations, and that is where I began to truly see my special abilities for what they were. I began to see the impacts one salty old soldier could have on a community, on a school, on a single child and elder. The veteran community has the capacity to shift our national values in a meaningful way, and I want to be a part of that. So, I am showing up and doing my best but it has not always been easy. When I re-entered college at ASU, I had a renewed sense of purpose, not only for myself but for my country.

Thanks to the support of my parents, who each now have a place in my life. Thanks to my Uncle David, who financially and spiritually carried me through the darkest of times. Thanks to my sister, who helped set a standard for me and hold me accountable. Thanks to all my family and close friends, who, whether they know it or not, helped me turn the page of my story and begin a new chapter.. Thanks to all of them, I graduated from ASU. An achievement that still makes me immensely proud of how far I have come in my journey.

I am a hard-headed veteran, and I know I am not the only one. If you are like me, take this as your call to arms. The call for you to reclaim that power which has always been inside of you. No matter if you have seen failure and defeat, no matter if you have given up in the past, no matter if you don't feel worthy. If you can read these words, it is not too late. Don't quit! Not yet!

I want you all to know you are worthy of the things you dream of and hunger for in your life. You deserve great things, but they will not come without effort and sacrifice. Wayne "The Great One" Gretzky once said, "You miss 100% of the shots you don't take."
Sports context: Wayne Gretzky was a hockey player from 1979 to 1999, hailing from Canada, but playing in the American NHL. Gretzky is the leading goal scorer, assist producer, and point scorer in NHL history, and has more career assists than any other player has total points. He is the only player to total over 200 points in one season—a feat he accomplished four times. In addition, Gretzky tallied over 100 points in 15 professional seasons, 13 of them consecutive. At the time of his retirement in 1999, he held 61 NHL records: 40 regular season records, 15 playoff records, and 6 All-Star records. To call him "The Great One" may be an understatement, nonetheless the greatest to ever play the sport. ***

Take your shots! Make them big! Move with haste. Apply for that job. Ask that person out. Send that email or text. Undertake the thing you've been dreaming about NOW. Get off the side line and get in the game, I promise, you'll have at least one cheerleader in me. But I will not be wearing pom-poms, just so you know.

I also want to make it clear I am not where I want to be myself yet. I still have more walls and mountains to overcome. I have personal dysfunctions, stemming from my PTSD that I am aware of, and I am sure there are some I am not aware of, but that just means I have more room for improvement. My progress in life is often sporadic, but that too can be the essence of consistency.

Stalwart Perseverance is the belief that not only are we all capable of redemption, but it is an essential part of development as human beings and leaders. The objective or desired outcome is not the point of the endeavor, but rather the process of not letting setbacks, failures, sabotage, or hardships defeat you, and instead viewing them as opportunities for growth and advancement.

The Great American Scream Machine

By Daniel Faust

Perseverance is built in two ways: living through pain or learning through others' pain. Which path is yours? A roller coaster is designed to thrill, excite, and scare. When you know you're going on one, you can prepare and even be excited for it. But when you're shoved into one of those rides, it can be a living hell for that entire time. Time freezes at that point. And I remember, when I was 10 to 12 years old, I was forced to go on a coaster Flume. This might be an East Coast thing. But this is a hybrid of a roller coaster and a flume. So, a water-based roller coaster—you get the speed in thrills while you're getting the effects of the water surrounding you, and you are drenched, to say the least. I was forced to be in front; I was yelling, screaming, and even bribing the controller at the top. When he pulled that switch, I yelled, "You suck!" all the way down in my 10 to 12-year-old little girlish boy's voice. The pain, the fear, the pressure was exhausting. Even though I had a little adrenaline rush, I never did that again.

My first seven years after leaving the military were very similar to the great American Scream Machine for me and my family. We're going to go through this in levels just like the ride, the momentum. The momentum started in my life just like the great American Scream Machine. It started when I did a cross-train to mental health. I thought the years of me being in it were going to be over. and that's information technology for you non-IT geeks. I thought leaving Information Technology for mental health would finally be the freedom that I needed to go do what God had called me to do. It was a start, but it was the wrong direction. From that point on, I went over and cross-trained and forced that cross-train to happen because the first year I was denied.

The second year I tried again and even asked the guy to basically waiver me in, and he did on the second year. I decided to cross-train in mental health, and everything started going haywire when I was in the tech school. I was having difficulty with the soft skills, while getting all the hard skills, but they wouldn't let me fail out of the school system. They said that I had to fail academically to leave the career field. I thought it was an integrity issue. It was probably God giving me a warning to say, "Hey, it's okay to fail in this season, because it's going to be a worse failure if you keep going." I didn't listen to that voice of wisdom. And I eventually passed the class.

I was the third highest grade point average in the class. I even got awarded, but then it got progressively worse. I located to Wright

Patterson Air Force Base, and I was having severe difficulty in the career field, just as they said I would. I could get all the hard skills, and the information, and memorize hundreds of definitions, but when it came to the soft skills of actually working with clientele, while balancing the hard skills of writing the notes in the medical format and meeting all the requirements, it was severely difficult. They thought they could train it into me. But that did not happen. A couple months later, as they were working with me. I busted my elbow during the military PT test. You could hear that ligament snap from a few hundred yards away. Come to find out, I had to get a surgery, and after getting the surgery and doing leave and coming back, I basically was told I was going to deploy. I said, "Really? You're gonna send me in this sling?" They said, "You got seven months. Seven months, Faust, you'll be fine." Well, physically, I became fine. I guess it's "fine is fine." Could be, but the deployment was a sham, to say the least. All my supervisors—didn't matter if they were NCO or senior NCO—tried to train those skills into me and to train the bad out of me. It didn't work.

When it came down to the deployment, I was fine for the first few days. But the thing of it was, I was doing progressively worse. When the new provider came in, they said "We're increasing our counseling load 300%. And you're gonna have to counsel patients, and write notes, and do all these things." And I'm thinking, "I've sucked at this thing for a long time for you to just train it out of me." Those words echoed through my soul again, and I was thinking, "This ain't gonna happen." And even though I tried my hardest to break that mindset, I couldn't grasp doing a 10-page medical note, getting all the answers to the questions, while still meeting the soft skills. Either I could be super-relational, and not get the paperwork done, or I could get the paperwork done and be cold. I remember one time I had providers thinking, "You, didn't get all the answers that we needed." But I'm thinking, "I caught the knife on the guy, and I knew he was security forces. And he and I had a great conversation." But the fact of the matter was, I didn't grasp both sets of skills. That perpetuated, so my commander, who was a gracious Commander, had lots of great meetings with me in the sand, literally, because when you're deployed, you're literally in the sandbox. But from there, they sent me home.

So, I went from what was to be a four- to six-month deployment to a roughly two-month one. I got home early, found out I had a vitamin D deficiency, and then hoped I would leave mental health and go back to calm. I did really well and was calm, but I was just burned out. And I thought helping people with their relationships and mental health status would be so much better, but I found out it was so much worse. I was struggling mentally. I was struggling emotionally. I was struggling spiritually. And now I'm back from this deployment, and my entire career is now struggling. I got a one EPR for my army and the rest of the folks. That's like getting the lowest rating on a performance report that you can get. The rest of my bullet points were fantastic. I helped the community and did all these things. I troubleshot all this computer stuff. I even taught classes, but two bullets of information—two lines—in a sea of paragraphs, I went over destroyed my active duty career at that point. I thought it was totally over. I had no chance to go over and be active duty again. That was the momentum that started the seven years of the Great American Scream Machine.

The first drop: as I was getting kicked out of active duty, I also got slammed with a big education bill when I was deployed and thought I was going to continue to be deployed. I was trying to set myself up for success. Just in case I had to get out of the service, I thought I was being wise by trying to get a web-design certificate—because everybody needed websites in 2012. It was booming. It's still booming in 2023. But the thing was, when you're in the Air Force and using educational benefits, you must start and complete the course by the time your enlistment is over. And, since my enlistment is getting cut short, the school gave me an extension, but the Education Center would not. So, I had to fork over $4,500 right before leaving the service. That was $900 a paycheck. It really slammed our family. But there was a little momentum during that time because I found out I was going to get severance pay. So, after the whole roller coaster happened about the education bill, and getting kicked out of active duty, we connected with a ministry. We thought we were gonna go to work with that ministry.

That ministry basically told me to slow down, take some time with my family, go get some connections, and then build some fundraising. But instead, I decided to move to the State where that ministry was located. And then to start my business called Perspectives and Reflections. I had a $17,000 severance. And I thought that plus unemployment was gonna stretch to support us. Well, I spent that money like crazy and thought I was spending it wisely. I even spent up to $500 a month on a specific advertisement for our first book. Come to find out, their advertising was targeting everybody from 18 to 65. **If you ever write a book, target your market.** So, from there, I just tried to do everything to get Perspectives and Reflections up and rolling.

As you're reading this right now, the name sounds kind of stupid, doesn't it? It sounds like a spa. God gave me the name, but I executed without His authority. And I eventually ran out of money, even though I hard charged and constantly pursued hundreds of churches and prospects and opportunities on social media and created content even in 2012 to 2013. We got to about September of 2012, literally just out of the

Air Force, roughly 60 days without pay. I was down to six weeks of pay, totally liquidated and destroyed. In that particular regard, I started aggressively applying for work. I was applying for work on two to 20 jobs a day at that point. We were down to $300, and then it got a little better. We were almost at the point that we thought we were going to be homeless, but I found out that I qualified as disabled and started getting money from the VA—roughly $700 at the time. So that was a big "Praise God!" Within a couple of days after that, I had jobs starting to compete for me. And I was actually excited because, again, I was starting to get work. Did I want to go back to work? No, I thought I had the calling to teach the world better relationships. You'll find out I still do. But at that time, I went back to work, so the job saved me. The first drop was over.

The second drop: I had the job that I got, which was in November and lasted for roughly five months. It was a great job for me at the time because I worked seven days on and seven days off. They were 12-hour days. They were long. One week I was on days; one week I was on nights, but the job was going great. So at least my boardroom was doing a little better. My girls were receiving disability, I was receiving disability. I had just gotten back into the reserves, which was sheer Providence at that time. That was in August, but I didn't know a second job was going to happen. During that time frame, my wife had some suicide attempts, and I lost that job a couple months later and was almost homeless for roughly six to seven months. I thought the drop was over when we finally got out of that state. And I'm saying, "Lord, I'm sorry. I pushed this. I tried to redeem the situation." Even in that time, God was providential. We were able to sell all our stuff, get out of that apartment that we lived in that state—Arkansas—get out of homelessness, and move back to the state where my wife came from—also one of my last active duty bases—Washington. So again, I thought, "Finally, it's rough, but we're done." If only that had been true!

The other drop—the loop the loop: So we moved to Washington, and it was great. Initially. We were able to rent a 500-square foot place, and we had a job. It had me traveling across the nation. I was back to working with the Navy and the Marines. Overall, it was a great job. Just as it was starting to get momentum again, within about 10 weeks of the job, a coworker of mine was the "Washington DC Naval Yard shooter"! He brought in three AK 47s, took out 12 people, and within a matter of a few hours, the job was "paused". About a week and a half later, they laid off 250 people. This was in 2013. It had been my first job getting back. We lived in Washington between 2013 and 2016. After that job went away, we got an eviction notice because that 500-square-foot place said, "Hey, you're gonna have to start paying and double dipping." So, we had to move to another place. This second place we moved into was a gorgeous 1600 square-foot place with two floors and a garage and was 80% the of my house dreams. But then that job went away, then other jobs also went away—a lot of jobs! We probably went through 30 to 40 jobs between 2013 and 2016. It was a real rollercoaster. But the hardest thing—why I call this section the "loop the loop"—was that my wife and I almost went through a full-on divorce.

I was an emotional wreck when we first got married. I said I believed in Jesus, but I didn't live it out in any practical way. I tried to gaslight her. If I was a filthy mouth, I tried to redeem the relationship with sex, candy and chocolates, and all the things that you think might rescue a marriage that seemed to be over—what you think might heal it. Well, that's everything but biblical. So, on my wife's birthday, either 2013 or 2014 (not sure of the specific year, just early in that program), we were going through another job—again. They said they were going to delete the contract because they thought it was going to be six months, but they only needed six weeks of work. My wife started arguing with me on the phone, and I essentially threatened divorce. And after hanging up, I started looking up how much a divorce would cost. At that moment, I was financially convicted. I wish I could say I was spiritually, philosophically, emotionally, practically, or in any other way, convicted, but I was only financially convicted… until I went home. When I went home that night, it was a three-hour spiritual, psychological, and emotional, nut-kicking. I had to learn to go back over everything, and I had to go through my mess—mentally, emotionally, socially, spiritually, intellectually. That "loop the loop" took so much out of me, because not only we were living in a state that I didn't want to live in, but also the job losses had taken their toll. And now my relationship was walking on eggshells each and every day while I'm working through all my junk. So that was the "loop the loop".

A second "loop the loop": I thought, the two drops in a "loop the loop" were enough, but I guess they weren't. Our second "loop the loop" was the remainder of the time that we were there, between 2014 to 2016. Our marriage was on a sort of "confidential fire insurance plan". Because she and I both had Jesus, we both stayed together. And we stayed for the kids. And we stayed for the finances, but emotionally, spiritually, sexually, and in every other way, we were operating on fumes. A lot of that time between 2014 and 2016, we were shoulder-to-shoulder, working on keeping a roof over our heads and looking for jobs. My wife went to culinary school during that time. I was doing military orders and almost went on deployment a couple of times because of that, but we were shoulder-to-shoulder, just keeping things surviving. At the end of that 2016 loop, as we went through roughly 30 to 40 jobs, we almost went through a third bout of homelessness. Each and every time that we endured this, after talking to financial advisors and everything else, the only conclusion was a lack of income. And that was what became the problem again between 2013 and 2016. I was on-again off-again orders, IT contracts that didn't last, and companies that ran out of money or were just not bringing in enough revenue.

At one point, I had six jobs cold in Arkansas. So, when orders run out and you don't have any IT leads, it's a place that you didn't want to be, but we were asking ourselves, "Do we sell our stuff again, and just reboot? Or do we stay here and try to fight the fight?" Our kids knew some of what we were going through, but not everything. So, we decided to move to the place where we really wanted to go, because even through the "loop the loops" and all of the rest of it, when we had the highs, we thought, "Where do we want to be?" Several months prior, before this bout of homelessness, I sent my wife on a trip to Arizona, specifically to Scottsdale, to check it out.

We were checking on a church, checking out the homes, and everything else. And it looked at that point like the grass was greener on the other side of the fence. My wife's migraines were better, and her general health was better. She has been spiritually free from all the stuff that she went through with the suicide attempts and all that that entailed. It was absolutely starting to get a lot better in marriage too. But, with that being said, we were about to become homeless again. So, do we stay, or do we go to Arizona and also try get jobs lined up? We decided to sell practically everything and get to Arizona. A shot of adrenaline! Things are finally starting to look up. We were able to sell everything. Things had been paid for in cash, so we got lots of money. I was able to sell for cash a baby grand piano, which somebody had given me for free. Someone gave us $300 to $500. I was able to sell the computer, the toys, and everything else so we got a shot of money into the account—thousands of dollars all at once! It's kind of scary when you go to the bank putting together that much cash into a deposit.

And when we got to Arizona, we were making good money. We were starting to rebuild. My health was a lot better. I didn't have as much back pain. I was able to get the vitamin D that I needed, the deficiency of which had basically destroyed me when I was deployed. But now I was in a place that was like my deployments. And my wife and I are feeling fantastic. We were able to move into a beautiful apartment that even had a pool, and everything else in our relationship was starting to get a lot better. That was a good time between 2016 to 2019.

One more Hill and drop: During 2018, most of you probably didn't feel this, but in the beginning of 2018, I was doing extremely well. I had just come to a border state. I was working government contracts; I was teaching and speaking across the nation; everything was improving. Then February 2018 came, and we had a CRA (a Continuing Resolution

Amendment) from the government. Under normal circumstances, when I was on military orders, this sort of thing could stop orders, or maybe pause them for a couple of days. But when that Continuing Resolution Amendment of February 2018 went through, all my contracts not only froze, they never became active again. Even though the people, in companies I wanted to work with, thought I was a great contractor/employee and even though I was getting paid $600 a day to teach and to speak (which is fantastic), all those contracts suddenly evaporated.

Also, in that timeframe (2017), I broke my back. Having just recovered from that, I was getting off military orders. Because of that, I had to learn how to walk again. Once I was finally able to walk again and was eligible to be a contractor, not only were contracts drying up on the government side, but the civilian contracts I had also washed away as well. So, 2018 was rough. I was working my business, working IT side hustles, and my wife was working at home. We were on food stamps and some other resources. Somehow, we survived 2018. We always look back at the close of each and every year. It seems that God has given us Providence, even through the drops, the "loop the loops", and all the rest of it; yet we were somehow climbing a hill again. At the end, we didn't know there was another drop coming. The year 2019 brought on-again, off-again orders, and other challenges. Specifically, I got a couple of sets of orders completed; then orders dried up. IT jobs dried up. I was advised that I owed more money on the government travel card than I anticipated. And then, I had my stripe taken away! So, I went from an E6 in the reserves to an E5 in late 2019 and couldn't get work, couldn't get jobs, couldn't get opportunities. And it was on this "hill and drop" that my wife and I really came together and started working jobs together for the first time. All the previous crap that we had gone through in 2013/2014 really sanctified us, bringing us together, as we both worked through our mess, asking God for healing and help. So, as I was grabbing an IT job, she came with me, and we started working together.

We worked in a ballot facility for about one and a half to two months. Then we worked in a taser and body cam factory together, and we were making really good money. But the downside of it was, that we were spending too much time away from our kids. And the possibility of homelessness kept popping up, primarily because these jobs were temporary. We got some grace in 2019. Earlier that summer, as I was going through the potential strike loss—which did happen—and then a bout of homelessness, we got an opportunity for a job for Dover Air Force Base. I had never thought that I would be thankful for a job at Dover Air Force Base. The prior year, I had worked there for six weeks, including through Christmas, but they were looking for workers, so I applied for government jobs in that area. And that is where this story has taken to us.

As of 2023, we are in a stable job. We've been in this job for three and a half years. And even though I don't like every aspect of the job, it has given me lots of opportunities to create things like this book, **Leave No Veteran Behind.** It has given stability to my kids and my wife, making it possible for her to create a ministry of her own. Our love, our sex, and our enjoyment of life has returned and has increased tenfold. And even the trials have gotten easier, this is just a small smattering of what these trials brought us, of the testimony we have been given, and of the fusing together of us in the calling of our lives. Three things arose out of all of this.

So, how does this apply? I want you to think about these as superhero tactics to build perseverance through learning. What three things do I, the 2023 Daniel Faust, wish that I could tell the 2012 Daniel Faust? (And I hope that you can take these in as "learn and live" things, as contrasted with "live and learn" things.

1. **Preparation will avoid the pain.** All of us, whether we're active duty, Guard or Reserve, have careers that will be over someday, and the military gives some good resources to set us up. But we need to set ourselves up for success. When I was in from 2000 to 2007, I blew probably between $50,000 to $150,000. If I had listened to some of the wisdom that other people gave me, and looked at other people, and prepared for life after active duty, even if I had saved $100 a month for the entire 12 years I was in, I would have had an additional $15,000 to $30,000 upon seperation.

1. Also, we tried to go into ministry right after we got out of active duty. It's a much better idea to take some time to plan or maybe work a part-time job for a while. I was getting told I needed to do these things to avoid the pain. I decided to do it otherwise. That's what caused a good amount of pain in the early stint. Preparation will avoid at least some of the pain. So, if you're still in the service, or you're still in as an employee, or wherever you're trying to go, you need to prepare so you can avoid the pain. A little bit of savings, an interim part-time job, waiting a while before getting that specific "nice thing", or not always going out to eat, can all help the transition. However, you do need to take care of yourself and have a small budget for fun. Even Dave Ramsey recommends a small budget for fun every couple of weeks to a month. That way, you don't go stir crazy. Prepare for the storms because storms will come. Don't assume everything's gonna be sunshine and rainbows, or that the grass really is greener on the

other side, or that you can orchestrate your life from the bedroom to the boardroom.

2. **Invest yourself wisely.** As military members, as veterans, or even as first-responders, you may read this book, you may hear this, and it all sounds a little weird. Let me break it down for you. The mission will go on without you. Do not put your Soul, your Life, your Strength, and your Energy into that war room or boardroom. Another way to say that is to invest in your spouse first. Invest in your family as an outpouring second. Then invest into that boardroom or war room third, because when push comes to shove, your war room or boardroom will go away. I had 70 different jobs between 2012 to 2019. Now I'm the extreme case, but on average in the first year to three years after you get out of the armed forces, you're going to find out that a job is going away, or in one way or another, something is going to happen. Or you're just gonna be sick and tired of being sick and tired. Your spouse and your kids are going to be that support system as you're going to need through these transformational moments. So, orchestrate your life, investing into the bedroom and into the living room first before you invest into the boardroom.

3. **Learn from the pain of others' wisdom.** I when I was looking at getting out of the service and wrestling with it, yeah, I had some good ideas. I tried to get a web design certificate. Okay, that was a thing that was unplanned and unwise. But at the time, I thought it was smart. But when I went to that ministry agency and said, "Hey, I want to apply to go and do this." They said, "Hey, you need to have 100 families." "Hey, you need to take a year with your spouse," "Hey, you need to get reacclimated into the civilian world. You need to find some civilian employment." I should have listened to that, because that advice was from the pain that they saw in the lives of people who had done it hardcore wrong over and over and over again. Sometimes, when you get denied an opportunity, it is a blessing in disguise. You can then build a perseverance to grow and eventually do it the right way.

2. So here are your tactics. Take what I'm doing when you want to go home and apply. And as you're reading the rest of this book, each of our people is going to give you these types of tactics. We hope and pray that this goes over and serves you and serves you well. Thank you for reading. See you in the next chapter.

Family Ties

Stefan Hobbs Jr.

When I was a young man, my dream, along with every other kid, was to become the next great athlete to ever play the game of football outside of the state of Florida. From the crack of dawn to the dimming twilight, the game of football held an unwavering grip on my heart and soul. It wasn't just a sport to me; it was my passion, my dream, and my first love. Each morning, as the sun rose, my mind immediately wandered to the gridiron. The excitement and anticipation of the day ahead filled my thoughts, setting the tone for the coming hours. The camaraderie among my teammates was a bond like no other. We formed a brotherhood, united by a common goal—to conquer the game and leave a lasting mark on the football field. The thrill of competing alongside like-minded individuals, each driven by the same burning desire for success, made every practice and game trip an unforgettable experience.

Those heated practices were more than physical exertion; they were the crucible in which champions were forged. In the crucible of sweat, determination, and sacrifice, I honed my skills, sharpened my mind, and pushed the limits of what I believed was possible. It was in those intense moments that the foundations of greatness were laid. The weather, at times harsh and unforgiving, added an element of challenge to my journey. Rain or shine, I embraced every condition Mother Nature threw my way. It was more than just adapting to the weather; it was an opportunity to prove my resilience and unwavering dedication. It was a reminder that greatness was not confined to ideal circumstances but thrived even in the face of adversity.

Growing up in Florida, I lived with my mother and stepfather. My mother was born and raised on the island of Guam. She was the rock and foundation of my family. She was the most supportive, loving, but intense disciplinarian I could've ever wanted. My Stepfather was born and raised in Florida and full of life. He loved sports and enjoyed music. They met in the early 90s while he was stationed in Guam. My stepfather served in the Marines for two years before being medically discharged. While it wasn't always easy, a bond of shared life experiences and resilience formed between them. The absence of my biological father, who was in Philadelphia and served in the United States Navy, cast a long shadow over the early stages of my childhood. It was like an eclipse. It seemed to dim the light of understanding, leaving behind a tapestry woven out of questions and what-ifs. The void created by his absence left an indelible mark, an ache that echoed in moments both big and small. It was a void that seemed to ask questions with no answers, leaving an imprint of yearning for a connection that felt like a puzzle piece missing from the whole. My uncertainty amplified my pain. Not knowing who my father was and if he wanted to be part of my life was a heavy burden. It was an emotional pendulum that swung between hope and despair, constantly tugging at my heartstrings. The longing for a connection became a paradox—the desire for his presence clashed with the fear of rejection. My mind raced daily with questions. Why did he leave? What does he look like? Was it something I did? The absence of answers compounded the pain, fueling a cycle of self-blame and unanswered inquiries.

As the seasons of my childhood unfolded, so did the complicated layers of family dynamics, revealing a mixture of conversations and gestures that spoke volumes beyond mere words. These silent nuances were like a hidden language, depicting complexity and hunger. The journey through this emotional labyrinth carried the weight of confusion and disbelief, yet it was driven by an unwavering desire for love and connection within the family's embrace. Unbeknownst to me, my biological father followed me well before we had any social media platform. During my senior year of high school, he contacted my school and told the administration staff that I was his son and would like to speak with me. He left his contact information behind to provide to my mother. I remember it like it was yesterday, walking into the house, when my mother and stepfather both said, "We need to talk." My parents sat me down in their bedroom and told me that my biological father contacted my school. You could hear a pin drop. So many emotions ran through my mind. I was shocked, happy, scared, and fearful of my response not to disappoint my parents. My initial reaction was that I did not want to talk with someone who never wanted to be in my life. I immediately regretted my response and spoke with him later the same evening. I remember hearing his voice for the first time. It was like talking to a celebrity. I knew this person existed, but I never thought in a million years that I would ever meet or speak to him. I remember crying myself to sleep that night asking God all the same questions all over again. Why did he never stay? Was it something I did? Did he ever love me?

My biological father tried to stay in contact, but his efforts were inconsistent with communication through letters. The closer I approached graduating high school, the more there was a moment when I anticipated meeting him for the first time. Again, my emotions were like a roller coaster. He wrote a letter asking if he could attend my graduation. Of course, I ran to my parents and told them I would love for him to attend. Unfortunately, he could not fly, so I worked a part-time job and saved every little penny to help purchase him a bus ticket through Greyhound. More pain and disappointment awaited me on the morning of my graduation. I recall waking up early that morning with my parents to pick him up from the bus station, only to receive an empty promise. He never showed up! I was immediately devastated. I hid all my pain during my graduation day. Everyone around me knew I was hurting and tried to keep me encouraged. I smiled but cried silently and grew more resentful. I received an apology letter roughly two weeks later from my biological father. He told me he sold the tickets to get high and was nervous to meet me. He was not ready to answer all the questions he knew I had readily prepared for him.

    In the absence of my biological father's guidance, the search for my identity became a complicated journey. Understanding my heritage, values, and character was challenging without his physical influence to provide insight into my family history and values. The quest led to a sense of displacement, feeling adrift between two halves of one's lineage. The question of "Who am I?" became uncertain as my father's absence prevented the complete montage of identity from taking shape. Having my own family, I understand why my mother was the way she was…she wanted the best for her children. Growing up with a stepfather who had served in the military brought unique challenges and experiences into my life. A military background in our home likely instilled values of discipline, honor, and dedication. My stepfather's service in the Marines and my mother's entrenched involvement influenced how I viewed the world lessons on the importance of sacrifice and commitment to a cause greater than myself. My stepfather and mother shared a standard core value of "family over everything."

    This shared belief became the cornerstone of our home, guiding how our family interacted and cared for one another. It emphasized the importance of unity, love, and support within the family unit. The value of "family over everything" meant that our family stood together as a united front in good times and bad. My stepfather and mother demonstrated this principle through their actions, often putting the family's needs ahead of their desires. Another important lesson I learned from my stepfather and mother was never to let my teammates or anyone down based on a lack of preparation. This ethos of responsibility and accountability extended beyond the boundaries of sports; it translated into all aspects of my life. This value of being reliable and dependable, understanding that my actions could have an impact on others, has been deeply instilled in my life. Growing up in a family where my parents did their best to care for one another while hiding any imperfection can create a perception of instability or division. As young men do, I compartmentalized much of my pain and frustration. So, I rarely spoke up or told my truth about my feelings because I never wanted to add drama or be an issue in a home filled with daily problems. However, unforeseen encounters arose as life unfolded, and unfamiliar obstacles disrupted the once solid foundation. Looking back in time, I wish I would have had more time on the practice field of life before I was thrown into the game.

As the days turned into months and the months into years, my love for the game of football only intensified. The ups and downs, victories, and defeats all contributed to my growth as a young man and an athlete. Football had become a way of life, etched into the very fabric of my being. With each passing day, my belief in the power of football to change lives grew stronger. It was no longer just about personal greatness or leaving a legacy on the field; it had evolved into something deeper and more meaningful. The game became a vessel through which I could support my family, get us out of the negative predicament, and still potentially connect with my biological father.

Graduating from high school and embarking on my college journey opened a new chapter in my life—one filled with opportunities and challenges. My journey from high school to college was undoubtedly filled with raw and unprotected emotions, shaped by the experiences I had growing up without the consistent presence of my biological father, due to his addictions and the unbalanced lifestyle with my stepfather and mother. As I ventured into this new phase, I began to grasp the reality that life is not as easy as it might have appeared before. My dreams and aspirations, including the desire to play football, were powerful motivators. Still, I also came to recognize bad decisions I made in the past had derailed my future aspirations. I often felt lost and unsure about what to do next. Nevertheless, other passions took root within me. I became overwhelmingly determined not to follow the same path as the fathers in my life. I craved to break the cycle of addiction and strive for a different, more fulfilling life for myself. This resolve fueled my decision to leave home at the age of twenty and set forth on a new path, independent and determined to create a better future.

Transitioning from the structured but unbalanced world of high school football, family dilemmas, and the uncertainties of adulthood was a puzzling experience. The desire to break the cycle of addiction and strive for a different life intensified daily, motivating me to seek something new. In 2003, in a world filled with turmoil, I decided to visit an Air Force recruiting office in Tampa, Florida. It was a pivotal moment that would change the course of my life. Joining the military was not something I had envisioned, but the need for change and a fresh start was undeniable. I recognized that I needed to make a quick decision to prevent myself from making more regrettable choices. This act of seeking a new direction showed my determination to take charge of my life and find a route that offered structure, discipline, and a sense of purpose.

Joining the Air Force took a few years to learn and adjust to the lifestyle. I felt more prepared to enter versus my lack of preparation for transitioning from childhood into young adulthood. Basic training became my new battleground, where the physical and mental challenges were reminiscent of my trials on the football field. The pain of my injuries, the longing for camaraderie, and the echoes of cheers from my past merged with the grueling routines of military life. As I pushed my limits, I discovered that the pain I had endured in my childhood and my sacrifices to join the military had uniquely prepared me for this moment. The camaraderie among his fellow Airmen felt like a familiar embrace, evoking memories of the brotherhood I had shared with my football teammates. When I entered the Security Forces Military Technical Training, I endured the rigors of training, finding strength in one another and a shared sense of purpose. The tears shed in moments of frustration and exhaustion were balanced by the sweetness of camaraderie, forming bonds that were unbreakable and reminiscent of the brotherhood. As the years unfolded, my journey through the military became a story of resilience, growth, and transformation. I embraced the challenges, rising through the ranks with a tenacity that mirrored my determination on the football field. The pain of my past became a driving force, propelling me forward as I faced obstacles with an unwavering resolve.

As the challenges of life abroad tested my resolve, I found myself facing a moment that would forever etch itself into my memory. This incident exemplified the depths of compassion and the power of human connection. A WORLD OF OPPORTUNITIES LAY BEFORE ME when I set foot on my overseas assignment. My friendship with my fellow airmen tempered the unfamiliar surroundings and the sense of being far from home. The shared experiences, mutual respect, and collective purpose formed a new kind of family that mirrored the bond I had known on the football field. In the Air Force, I discovered that the lessons I imbibed from my football days were not in vain. The discipline, teamwork, and resilience I had honed on the field seamlessly translated to the demands of military life. I approached my duties with a sense of purpose, determination to excel and to lead by example. All my learned experiences came together at one critical time of leaving no veteran behind.

It was a frigid evening. The temperature was a negative five degrees, with heavy winds cutting through my clothing. I was comfortably at home relaxing. I was watching a movie called "The

Magnificent Seven" when I received an unexpected and chilling phone call that shook everything inside and dropped everything I was doing "instantly." The call was at approximately 19:14 hours. A fellow teammate was on the brink of despair, teetering on the edge of a precipice that seemed insurmountable. The words pierced through the phone line were a cry for help, a desperate plea that echoed in the depths of my consciousness. I felt every sense of pain my friend was enduring at that moment, the intensity of his voice screaming out for someone to show up. It was a call that carried a weight beyond measure. His voice reverberated with emotions that transcended distance. In an instant, everything changed. The movie's entertaining narrative was overshadowed by the gravity of the situation unfolding at the other end of the line. It was as though time itself stood still, frozen by the urgency of the words that pierced through the phone's connection. My heart and mind simultaneously linked and dropped in fear of the unexpected within the next few minutes.

    My teammate had been a man of few words, his actions speaking louder than the syllables he chose to utter. He was the embodiment of strength, which didn't require grand gestures or vocal affirmations. His stoicism was his armor, a shield that protected him and those around him. But that armor, it seemed, had its chinks, and in that vulnerable quiver of his voice lay evidence that even the strongest among us have their breaking points. In a split second following that chilling call, a primal instinct surged within me, the age-old dichotomy of fight or flight. But within that critical moment, there was no hesitation, no wavering. The protector within me sprang into action, eclipsing any doubts and fears that might have lingered in the shadows. The choice to leap into action wasn't conscious; it was a response driven by a surge of adrenaline and unwavering resolve.

    I was always taught within Security Forces to react swiftly and decisively in the face of adversity, and now, those instincts were put to the ultimate test. Abandoning all other concerns, I raced to his friend's residence, my heart pounding as the gravity of the situation weighed heavily on my shoulders. The night air was thick with tension, and the scent of rain lingered as I arrived at my colleague's doorstep. His phone calls had gone unanswered, and a sense of dread settled over me like a heavy shroud. The silence was deafening as I entered the residence; anguish and despair unfolded before his eyes. I thought I was too late. I arrived to see my brother lying on the floor, with a pistol in hand, his eyes filled with tears and pain. My training and instincts kicked into high gear as I reached for my phone to call for medical assistance while attempting to provide comfort and support for my brother.

    I navigated the situation with compassion, authority, and unwavering support. I was able to empathize with him because of the challenging moments in my life that were never addressed. Being there and speaking positively reminded him that he was not alone and that some people cared deeply for his well-being. The incident marked a turning point in my life, encapsulating the essence of my ability and the values I had cultivated throughout my journey. I realized in that moment this could've been me in this situation. Looking back on all my mental and emotional trauma, I realized how much I suppressed from childhood until my early thirties. I was in denial; I knew how to disguise my flaws to people. I knew how to put my false representation out for people to be pleased but never asked for help when I needed it the most, because I learned at an early age how to bury my feelings from those I called family. I can call it ego, pride, arrogance, ignorance, or all the above. It was my reality check; I wish my brother never placed himself in that situation. My brother tells me thank you for showing up for him that night, and in return, I tell him thank you for showing me how to be strong without fear. **We saved each other's lives that night.**

    He showed me his courage that night and called me without fearing being judged or consequences. I was more prepared to provide aid for my teammates and continue to neglect my blind spots and not think twice about exposing my vulnerabilities for support. My journey with the Lord unfolds in a series of chapters, each revealing a layer of understanding, a depth of connection that transcends the ordinary. There are moments when my life's complexities align, the heavens open up, and God's presence becomes palpable. During these moments, I have been called to action to be a vessel of His love and compassion in a world that often craves both. I have been actively engaged in my journey with the Lord. God has a miraculous way of getting our attention when we least expect it.

    I am thankful to God for blessing me and keeping me near the cross with His hand of protection. God created a space for me to have a family, a beautiful wife, and a son. God's love is my anchor, a foundation upon which I can build my hopes, dreams, and aspirations. My beliefs encourage me to approach each day with gratitude, recognizing the blessings present even during challenges. It's a reminder that the love of God is not confined to a single moment or circumstance; instead, it is a constant presence that sustains and nurtures. The camaraderie I've experienced as a child has evolved into a profound sense of brotherhood within the Air Force, a brotherhood that extends beyond geographical borders.

    My decision to join the military was undoubtedly one of the best decisions I've ever made. It offered an opportunity to find purpose, camaraderie, and a sense of belonging in a community dedicated to something greater than oneself. The military allowed me to channel my energy and determination into a noble cause, and it became a platform for my strengths and talents to shine. As I reflect on my journey, it's evident that the desire to break free from the past and create a different life for myself was the catalyst that led me to the military. My decision to venture into the unknown and embrace the challenges of military life demonstrated courage and resilience.

During my twenty-year journey in the military, it has been a tapestry woven with a mix of extraordinary moments and complex challenges. My experiences have taken me to beautiful countries, exposed me to diverse cultures, and provided unforgettable memories. My military experience has undoubtedly offered a unique opportunity that few others experience. Amidst the highs, there has also been deep sadness and loss. The military demands sacrifice, and the ultimate cost can be the loss of comrades and friends. These tragic moments have left a lasting impact on my heart, and the pain they bring does not quickly fade away, if ever. While the military journey has been filled with joy and camaraderie, it's essential to recognize and honor the emotional toll it takes. The pain of loss and separation is a testament to the deep connections formed during service, and it reflects the dedication and love I have for my fellow service members and loved ones. During those difficult times, I often encourage and recommend my teammates to lean on the support of those around them and fellow servicemembers who understand our unique challenges, friends who stand by us, and family who eagerly await our return home. I remind them it's okay to grieve and to feel the weight of the sacrifices made. Emotions are a natural response to the experiences we've endured. We must find healthy ways to cope with the pain, such as talking with a counselor, participating in support groups, or engaging in activities that bring comfort and joy.

As I continue to navigate through life, I choose to surround myself in the presence of good people and pay it forward. The encounters I have endured have profoundly impacted me, as their words and actions have been embedded into my heart and soul, sowing seeds of wisdom and inspiration that have borne fruit within my spirit. In the Bible, Zechariah 8:12 says, "For the seed shall be prosperous, the vine shall give its fruit, the ground shall give her increase, and the heavens shall give their dew." Zechariah reminds us of the abundant blessings that God bestows upon those who seek Him and follow His ways. As leaders our daily purpose is to positively sow seeds into people in the military and our community and families. Every leader has experienced a significant amount of their own obstacles. Nevertheless, we must display the accuracy of commitment, dedication, honor, sacrifice, and excellence. **It's our turn!** Our responsibility is to lead and provide positive stewardship for the next generation of men and women serving our military.

Although I never had the chance to meet my biological father in person, the family legacy lives on through my son and I, who both carry the family name. Sharing my experiences provides solace, and it's part of my purpose to pay it forward. The absence of my biological father's presence does not diminish the desired connection that I always wanted to have with him and the impact he has had on my life. It is a testament to the enduring power of family ties and my deep sense of responsibility and love toward my son. I unconsciously followed my father's footsteps by joining the military. This promise echoes the values instilled by my family who prioritized family over everything. I understand the profound importance of being there for my children, providing them with love, support, and guidance as they navigate life's journey. As I continue to embrace my father and military leader role, I vow never to leave my children behind or forgotten. Being a parent is a sacred responsibility, and I am determined to fulfill it with unwavering dedication. I will strive to be the best father I can be, always ready to face the challenges and joys of parenthood with an open heart. The family name I share connects me to a lineage that stretches back through generations, and I carry the weight of that heritage with pride. The name represents not just my biological father but all those who came before him, shaping the person I am today. I will never leave you behind or forget you, Pop. Love you!

Oceans of Wisdom

By Kurt Porter

This is the journey of how a Seaman Recruit who served in the United States Navy during the height of the Cold War ends up fulfilling his dream of working, living, and coming to own his own successful business in Russia. There were many lessons learned along the way, both good and bad.

Defense Language Institute, NSGA Clark AFB, Philippines, Special Projects

During May, a long time ago, in a city far, far away, a high school sophomore, along with his Spanish class, visited the Defense Language Institute (DLI) on Language Day in Monterey, California. He fell in love with DLI and the Monterey Peninsula. The foreign foods, the dancing, the skits, and seeing all the military students speaking fluently in a foreign language was amazing. He told himself as a 15-year-old, "When I turn 18, I'm going to join the Navy and learn a language at DLI."

So, I did. This one visit changed my life immensely, setting me off on an incredible, unforgettable journey. It exposed me to 80+ different countries, cultures, ways of life and provided me the opportunity to meet and make many good friends. DLI Language Day is military propaganda at its finest. I'm so glad I was lucky enough to visit DLI while in high school and fall for that military trap!

After graduating from Boot Camp, I was sent to DLI for the Basic Vietnamese Course, which was a 37-week course. The course was a very intensive six hours a day in class, and two-three hours of homework daily. Upon graduation, I attended follow on training at Goodfellow Air Force Base for a 16-week Technical Language Course (C School).

Post-Goodfellow, I was transferred to the Philippines where I served four wonderful years at Clark Air Force Base. I was in a Direct Support (DIRSUP) assignment at the Naval Security Group Activity (NSGA Clark), as a Naval Airborne Cryptologist.

What does that mean? I cannot provide many details because the job was classified. However, I deployed to a lot of different ships including aircraft carriers, frigates, and destroyers. I flew on EP3-Orion Aircraft as well as on EA-3B Sky Warriors, which were launched from aircraft carriers. The A-3 was a 7-seater and was the largest aircraft flown from an aircraft carrier. It was affectionately known as the "Whale." I was fortunate, as my Vietnamese was excellent, to also serve as an interpreter during Vietnamese Boat People rescue operations in 1979 and 1980. This was very heady and challenging work for a 20-year-old, but it was also extremely gratifying.

After serving my initial enlistment of four years, I decided to reenlist and return to Monterey for the 47-week Basic Russian Course. I started my Russian studies in January of 1983.

I think this second time at DLI is where I learned one of my primary life lessons. Maybe even a shocking truth for me—*You get out of **any** endeavor **only** what you put into it.* I'm talking about spent time and effort. My parents tried to teach me this truth, but I'm stubborn. It took failures both in military and civilian life to truly understand this truth and to make it part of my personal philosophy.

At DLI again, I was 22 years old, and my former spouse was a young lady from the Philippines who was an immigrant and was having difficulties adjusting to a new life in the States. It was difficult for her to leave her family and friends behind to encounter this new country and new culture. Unfortunately, I didn't have a lot of time to help her make the adjustment, because I was very involved in trying to study for the Petty Officer First Class exam, and I had a tremendous amount of military collateral duties to go along with my Basic Russian Studies.

Something had to give, and for me, it was doing the homework for my Basic Russian Course. Approximately six weeks into the course, I went to my teacher and said, "I'm not going to do any more homework."

She looked at me and she said, "Well, I'll tell your Command." I replied, "Go ahead. All they'll do is send me back to the Philippines, where I had a really good time, and my wife is comfortable." She looked at me and said, "Okay, just study for all the tests. If you get A's, you don't have to do the homework."

On one hand, that was a tremendous relief. It freed up a couple of hours every night. On the other hand, I realized it was one of the stupidest decisions that I'd ever made in my life. I graduated the course with honors, but I cannot say that I really had a good feel for the Russian language at that time.

When I got to Goodfellow Air Force Base to study the follow-on technical portion of the language training, I made a commitment to work very diligently. There, I laid the foundation to become a decent Russian speaking cryptologist, which is going to bring us to another lesson learned for me in my military service: there's more to being a military linguist than just military vocabulary and terms. An outstanding base in the studied target language is extremely important!

The following year, while flying with Special Projects out of Brunswick, Maine, our squadron was assigned to fly over a Soviet submarine that had made an emergency ascent and was on fire. Without getting into any classified details, while I did an okay job, all the nonmilitary, pure Russian language vocabulary sort of kicked my rear.

I realized I should have put more time into my studies of the Russian language while at DLI. I swore to myself that I would never let that happen again. I promised myself that if I ever went back to language school, I would study and do all my homework.

After completing my tour with Special Projects, I returned to Monterey for Intermediate Russian, which was a 42-week course. Even though the Intermediate Russian Course didn't have a lot of homework, I made sure that I created my own homework to do after the six-hour day of academics. I put in two to three hours every night on various subjects. Russian grammar, vocabulary, reading articles, short stories, novels, watching movies, listening to music, listening comprehension, I did it all. This really helped improve my Russian a great deal, as after graduating from the Russian Intermediate Course, I received outstanding scores on the Defense Language Proficiency Test, or the DLPT, and the Navy proposed that I stay in Monterey for the next three years to serve as a Military Language Instructor (MLI).

I was lucky enough to share an office with two Russian instructors. I made another commitment to myself. I was not going to speak English with them ever. I was not going to speak English with any of the Russian instructors. I was going to speak Russian and "force" them to speak Russian with me.

Sure enough, a lot of the Russian Language Instructors wanted to speak English with an MLI thinking, "Well, he's an American; he's going to speak English." It would have been good practice for them. Nope. I was going to be selfish and go another way. I pushed and pushed and pushed. Finally, all the Russian Native Speakers understood, if you wanted to talk to me, you were going to have to speak Russian. Sitting with my friends Boris and Ilya, plus committing to speak Russian with Russian Native Speakers improved my Russian language skills immensely. Please don't forget: *You get out of **any** endeavor **only** what you put into it.*

After a year of teaching at DLI, Presidents Reagan and Gorbachev signed the Intermediate Range Nuclear Forces (INF) Treaty. The Department of Defense went on an immediate search to find Russian speaking military linguists to serve as escort interpreters for Soviet Inspection Teams in the United States, or inspector interpreters for American Inspection Teams in the Soviet Union. To make a long story short, an already super assignment at DLI turned into the best job in the world. I taught Russian daily, and twice a year I went to the Soviet Union to interpret during the elimination of Treaty Limited Items or during quota inspections. During my first trip to the Soviet Union in January of 1989, I asked myself, "What would my Russian be like if I lived here for five years? Someday, I'm going to move here and find out." That dream would take many years to fulfill.

During my tour at DLI, I also escorted Soviet Inspectors 3-4 times per year during the rest of my assignment. DLI Monterey was very good to me. My professional achievements included: Completing a 2-week intensive interpreting course at the U.S. State Department with its top two Russian interpreters, selection as the Naval Security Group Detachment Sailor of the Year, Military Language Instructor of the Year (#1 of 81 MLIs), awarded a Joint Service Commendation Medal, and a promotion to Chief Petty Officer. *You get out of **any** endeavor **only** what you put into it.*

On-site Inspection Agency (OSIA), Travis Air Force Base, California, Naval Reconnaissance Support Detachment, (NRSD) Misawa, Japan

My next duty station was at Travis Air Force Base in California, where for three years, I served as an Escort Interpreter for Soviet/Russian Inspection and as Deputy Team Chief for various arms control inspections within the United States. In addition to fulfilling my leadership and management obligations, I continued to improve and refine my Russian Language, and interpretation and translation skills. OSIA offered a wide variety of language sustainment and enhancement courses. At the end of the tour, I was promoted to Senior Chief Petty Officer first time up, and I was offered the position of Command Senior Chief at the Naval Reconnaissance Support Detachment in Misawa, Japan.

Things changed a lot for me because for the previous five years, I had served in a pure Russian language environment. I had spent my time interpreting, translating, escorting, inspecting, and I had been away from the Naval cryptologic world.

I was now Command Senior Chief of a 70-person detachment, the Commanding Officer's right hand, if you will. The liaison between the enlisted force and the Commanding Officer. Five Chief Petty Officers reported to me. I also flew on missions off the coast of Russia.

While I was in Misawa, the U.S. Navy and the Russian Navy decided to start of program of exchanging port visits. The U.S. Navy made several port visits to Vladivostok, Russia. I trained most of the Naval Cryptologists that supported those visits over a two-year period in interpretation and translation techniques.

The Naval Airborne Cryptologic mission, as far as Russian linguists were concerned, had deteriorated. After the Cold War ended, the Russian Navy cut way back on the construction of new ships, the repair and restoration of its then current battle order, and as a result, deployments out to sea. The Russian Air Force flew very rarely. Work became very boring, honestly. It was indeed a challenge to motivate young sailors when the job didn't seem that exciting to them. The trips to Vladivostok helped us keep some of the better linguists motivated and trained.

I enjoyed these port visits to Vladivostok. What an incredibly beautiful city! While I don't agree with the idea of many "Vladivostoktsi" that their city is the San Francisco of Russia, there are indeed similarities: a beautiful bay, rolling hills, and some architecture. I visited Yul Brenner's childhood home during one of these port visits.

With the Cold War over, the Navy offered early retirement to Senior Chief Petty Officer Russian linguists. I decided to retire two years early, getting out at 18 years of service. The only benefit I lost was a 2% reduction in retirement pay. It didn't matter. I knew in my heart that I wanted to do something with my Russian language. I didn't want to lose my language skills. It was an easy choice to make the transition from military to civilian life.

On-Site Inspection Agency/Defense Threat Reduction Agency

After retiring from the Naval service, I returned to Suisun, California, which is near Travis Air Force Base. I applied for both government jobs and jobs in the private sector. I received a job offer with the then On-site Inspection Agency as a Russian Language Instructor in the Open Skies Division. Within a year, I became Chief of the Language Training Branch. I had five Russian native speakers working for me. Our function was to provide language and interpreter training to over 145 Russian-speaking military linguists and Foreign Area Officers. We also taught treaty courses: the INF Treaty, START Treaty, Open Skies Treaty, and the Nuclear Treaties.

I was also in charge of the interpreter selection and training process for military-to-military missions (Russian/American contacts for other than Arms Control support). A year after I started my job at OSIA, the agency combined with two other major commands to become the Defense Threat Reduction Agency.

George C. Marshall Center, Garmisch, Germany

My third year with OSIA/DTRA, I saw that a job had opened in Garmisch, Germany. Even though it was a step back to go from a GS-13 to a GS-12 position, I applied for and took the job because it had been a goal to live in Germany for some time. The Marshall Center is in Bavaria at the foot of the Bavarian Alps. With housing and a cost-of-living allowance provided, it wasn't a difficult decision to make the move overseas again. Little did I know that this assignment was the final steppingstone to finally moving to Russia.

Over the next seven years, I worked as the Marshall Center's Registrar, Deputy Director for the Partnership for Peace Defense Academy and Security Studies Institutes (located within the Marshall Center), and became the Chief, Language Services Branch. I was a GS14 simultaneous interpreter, interpreting from English to Russian and Russian into English, primarily during electives and then during consecutive interpreting while on field studies at governmental institutions in Europe and the United States.

I was responsible for the management of 20+ staff interpreters/translators and over 50 contractors. This assignment allowed me to continue to hone my skills in interpretation and translation. This was an assignment to remember, a combination of leadership, management AND using my Russian language.

While I was at the Marshall Center, I supported an extensive number of military-to-military contacts as a team leader and interpreter. If there were European Command Naval, Army, and Air Force representatives participating in joint exercises, planning meetings, or conferences with their Russian military counterparts, European Command called upon the Marshall Center to provide them with interpretation and translation support. Thanks to this work, I made a lot of solid contacts within European Command and the U.S. Embassy in Moscow.

Parsons Global Services and Chelyabinsk and Moscow Russia

One summer day in 2006, while in Moscow for Marshal Center sponsored language training, something lucky occurred that again adjusted my life's direction. I was in a two-week course at Moscow State University. On this fine Saturday, I just happened to be walking around Izmailovsky Park, an outdoor flea market that is open all year round. You can get various Russian souvenirs at this flea market at a decent price.

One of my former students/colleagues screamed at me, "Kurt, Kurt, what are you doing here?" He's an excellent amateur photographer; he was taking some shots in the flea market. He was stationed at the Defense Threat Reduction Agency in DC. At the time of our chance meeting, he was in Russia temporarily supporting the Chemical Weapons Destruction Support Office, which was located at the U.S. Embassy in Moscow.

He informed me that there was a potential job for me in Chelyabinsk Russia, which is in the Ural Mountains. Parsons Global Services was looking for an English-language editor to edit translations done by Russian natives from Russian into English. The Russian translators, while being excellent translators, had some issues translating into their non-native language. There's always going to be mistakes in grammar, syntax, spelling, and punctuation for almost any translator who is required to translate into their non-native language. It's much easier to translate into your native language.

This was a government contract. PARSONS Global Services was managing executing the contract for my former employer the Defense Threat Reduction Agency, which signed this contract as an agreement with the Russians to build Chemical Weapons Destruction Facility in Shchuch'ye which was in the Kurgan Region, an hour and a half from the city of Chelyabinsk.

I applied for the job and underwent an extensive interview and testing process. Within a year, I became the Director of

Communications, which meant that 20 different translators and interpreters in several different divisions reported to me. I performed quality control of their work, and additionally, I interpreted during high-level discussions between the Parsons Vice-president in charge of the Project, as well as for senior U.S. government DTRA representatives when they came to Russia to meet their Russian Counterparts. The best part of the whole deal? Becoming the Director of Communications also included an increase in salary and a move to the Parsons Global Services Moscow Office!

Parsons Global Services and Quality Translations Services International, Moscow, Russia

Seventeen years after asking myself what my Russian would be like if I lived in Russia for five years, I'd already spent a year living in Chelyabinsk, Russia working in the private sector, and I was now living in one of the finest capital cities in the world. Restaurants, bars, nightclubs, theater, opera, art galleries, shopping, every type of museum under the sun. Parks galore. I immensely enjoyed working for Parsons and living in this urban paradise. Yes, I burned the candles at both ends. I totally immersed myself in the culture and all that Moscow had to offer.

However, something was missing. I wanted more. Even though I had an extremely nice compensation package with Parsons, I wanted to make more money. No less important, I had a burning desire to create something from the ground up. I wanted to be the boss and call the shots. I decided to continue to burn the candles at both ends, albeit in a more positive fashion.

A logical conclusion was for me to keep my day job and form my own company on the side. For a 2-year period, I worked eight hours a day for my company, and then I worked out of my bedroom at night. I made **$1.2 million** during this timeframe between the two enterprises.

I started by forming my own company. Building a company is a multifaceted and challenging endeavor that involves numerous key steps and considerations. Here is a general roadmap to help you navigate the process of building a successful company. I will share with you what I thought I did well as I navigated my own journey, and I will share with you my failures. More importantly, I will explain the "why," via anecdotal reinforcement points, which will be in italics.

1. Idea Generation and Validation:

- Start by identifying a business idea or concept. This could be based on a personal passion, a market gap you've identified, or a unique solution to a problem.
- Conduct market research to validate your idea. Analyze market trends, competition, and customer needs to ensure there's demand for your product or service.

Right up front, you should immediately draw up a list of what you have to offer. I knew I was going to create a service-based virtual company. At this point in my life, my strengths were in program management, public speaking, knowledge of the Russian language, interpretation and translation, and teaching and facilitating. It made the decision easy. I decided to open a Translation Agency. Quality Translations International was born! Well, it was an idea.

My initial goal was to obtain contracts for both commercial and governmental interpretation and translation services. I planned on utilizing all the contacts I had developed when I was in the military and working in the Federal Service. I also wanted to capitalize on being the lone native English-speaking military interpreting expert in the private sector who lived in Moscow.

2. Business Plan:

- Create a comprehensive business plan that outlines your company's vision, mission, goals, and strategies.
- Include financial projections, marketing plans, operational details, and a SWOT analysis to assess strengths, weaknesses, opportunities, and threats.

A good business plan is the foundation of any company. I used my business plan to create my marketing plans, marketing materials, and shape my pitch presentations. If you don't have a vision, know your mission, and what your goals are, you're not off to a good start. This was a positive for me.

This was a <u>major</u> weakness. While I did a decent job with my initial marketing plans and financial projections, I did not do a proper SWOT analysis. This led to weaknesses in other business development and sustainment areas. I did not properly evaluate markets other than my initial goal of military markets.

3. Legal Structure and Registration:

- Choose a legal structure for your company (e.g., sole proprietorship, LLC, corporation) based on your specific needs and goals.
- Register your business with the appropriate government authorities and obtain any necessary licenses or permits.

Your specific needs and goals should also include your tax goals. Different structural entities have pros and cons when it comes to how and what types of taxes a company pays. I registered my company as a sole proprietorship located in the state of Delaware.

Figuring out registration, licensing and permits can be a complex. I decided to outsource these activities. I went with Legal Zoom. You can get some free services with them, but I paid $750 for a comprehensive registration package. They handled everything. I was so satisfied with their services; I used them again recently to form a new business venture. They can be found at legalzoom.com. Knowing I wanted to bid for and win government contracts, I obtained a DUN number and registered in the official U.S. Government Contractor Database.

4. Funding and Financing:

- Determine how you'll finance your business. Options include personal savings, loans, investors, or crowdfunding.
- Create a detailed budget to manage your start-up and ongoing expenses.

After developing my budget to manage my start-up costs and projecting my ongoing expenses, I knew that I'd be able to establish my company using personal savings.

5. Branding and Marketing:

- Develop a strong brand identity, including a company name, logo, and messaging.

- Create a marketing plan that includes strategies for reaching your target audience through advertising, social media, content marketing and other channels.

While I did fine with the website that I created using Go Daddy, my primary lesson learned was to not go cheap. Branding and marketing are so important today. It's essential to take advantage of all the advertising tools that are available.

Unless you have extensive experience in marketing, I recommend you use a company to help you get started. For my latest business venture, I went with https://thestartupstreet.com/ While this company is not inexpensive, its products and services are extremely high quality, and its guidance is top notch. They have my highest recommendation.

6. Product/Service Development

- If you're offering a product, design, prototype, and manufacture it.
- If you're offering courses, develop them.
- If you're offering a service, establish the processes and train your team.
- Focus on quality and customer satisfaction.

This point was a success for me. I developed several courses to provide immersion training for U.S. military linguists in Moscow. On the translation side, I built up a database of 75+ freelance translators and interpreters.

7. Team Building

- Recruit and hire skilled individuals who align with your company's values and goals.
- Establish clear roles and responsibilities within your team.

I found highly skilled and professional instructors for the various courses that I developed. I ensured they understood my expectations for quality. I trained them in the teaching methodology that I knew the U.S. Department of Defense desired.

Regarding the freelance translators I hired, I trained them on how the assignment process would flow, and I laid out my expectations for quality both verbally and in writing.

I developed Client Surveys for both the teaching and translation sides of my company. I wanted to ensure that we were meeting their needs, and the surveys were a tool to get feedback. In addition, I called my respective points of contact monthly to touch base and to inquire if there was anything we could do from their perspective to improve our services.

8. **Sales and Distribution**

- Develop a sales strategy to promote and sell your products and services.
- Consider different distribution channels and partnerships to reach a broader audience.

While I did well with bullet one in this area initially, I failed to develop a sales strategy for sustainment. While I did have a couple of partners who help me reach a larger audience, I should have looked for more. It goes back to the adage of "Plan your work and work your plan." However, as a CEO you should be asking yourself, "Do I need to adjust the plan? Is it time to tweak it? Is this plan valid for not only our current tasks, but does it allow us to grow and evolve?".

9. **Operations and Systems:**

- Implement efficient operational processes and systems to streamline your business operations.
- Invest in technology and tools that can help you manage and scale your company.

Remember, bigger is not always better. Especially when you are starting out. Make sure that you have the proper level of administrative, financial, and logistical support for your scopes of work. Expanding too soon can lead to unnecessary expenses. Expanding too late can lead to possibly not being able to complete a job or meet contractual requirements with the required quality.

10. **Financial Management:**

- Monitor your financial performance regularly.
- Maintain accurate financial records and accounting practices.
- Adjust your budget and strategies as needed to ensure profitability.

As I began my business, I handled these on my own using commercially available software. As the business grew, I hired both an administrator and an accountant. This was both a success and failure for me. The success was I was able to save some money at the start-up by doing it myself. The failure was that I didn't recognize the money I was saving didn't make up for the money I should have been earning by obtaining new business.

11. Growth and Scaling:

- As your company grows, explore opportunities for expansion, including entering new markets, launching new products, or acquiring competitors.
- Be prepared for scalability challenges and adapt your systems and team accordingly.

This was my single largest failure as a CEO and greatest lesson learned. I only had three primary clients, 1) European Command 2) the U.S. Embassy Moscow 3) a Houston-based translation agency that was sub-contracting an oil and gas translation project to my company. While there was lots of small work coming in, unfortunately, I had all my eggs in one basket. While that was the market that I aimed for at my company's start-up, I should have expanded my Client Base. I will elaborate in my primary lessons learned at the end.

12. Customer Relationship Management:

- Build and nurture strong relationships with your customers.
- Collect feedback and use it to improve your products or services.

I covered this in Point 7 (Teamwork). The only thing I would add is that when you collect feedback to improve, don't limit it to your clients. You hired your staff for a reason. Their input on the product and services could prove invaluable. Be ready for constructive feedback.

13. Legal and Compliance:

- Stay informed about legal and regulatory requirements relevant to your industry.
- Comply with tax laws, employment regulations and intellectual property rights.

Even if you formed your company as I recommended in Point 3 (Legal Structure and Registration), I recommend you speak with the company that helped you register at least twice a year to make sure there are no changes to bullets one and two of this Point.

14. Continuous Learning and Adaptation:

- Be open to learning from your experience and adapt your strategies based on market feedback and changing circumstances.

15. Exit Strategy (not mandatory):

- Consider your personal long-term goals as well as your company's. This could involve selling the business, going public, or passing it on to a successor.

Primary Lessons Learned

You've got to absolutely diversify your client base. My company, while it made a ton of money in a very short time, was not a sustainable business model. One should never make more than 15% of his profits from any one client. One day you're sitting high and mighty. The next day, the oil and gas markets have crashed, and the end client has fired all the foreigners that worked on the project and are now handling everything with local nationals—no translation services required. Or the country you live in has invaded another country and the U.S. military is no longer engaged in cooperation with this country. The more diversified you are, the better you'll be able to adapt to ever-changing markets.

The roadmap works! However, as a CEO you need to review it constantly to make sure you're staying on the path. *You get out of **any** endeavor **only** what you put into it.* This applies to consistently applying all points of the roadmap.

Diversification of revenue streams. Take some of your profits and put them into other businesses. Preferably something with long-term passive income.

Conclusion

Building a company is a dynamic and ongoing process that requires dedication, resilience, and a willingness to learn and adapt. Surround yourself with mentors and advisors who can provide guidance along the way and remember that success often comes with persistence and a commitment to delivering value to your customers and stakeholders. Some people say, "It's better to be good than lucky." I say, "You make your own luck."

Authors' Contact Information

(Not every author has provided contact information. Those listed here are the ones who have.)

Yesenia Vazquez-Rosa   (Saying "Yes" to You)

Demetrius Booth   (I See Men as Trees)

Granny Lisa Kraft   (Sharing the Pain)

Mike Montiel   (You Are Worthy)

Daniel Faust   (The Great American Scream Machine)

Kurt Porter   (Oceans of Wisdom)

Author Contact Information

Yesenia Vazquez-Rosa, Founder & Owner YESpreneur & Blue Coastal Homes

Email yesenia@yesprenuer.com or mailto:myesenia@bluecoastalhomes.com

Instagram: @coach_yesenia | @yesprenuer_ | @bluecoastalhomes

Facebook: @yesenia Vazquez-rosa | Blue Coastal Homes | YESprenuer
Tags: Author, Coach, Publisher, Entrepreneur, Investor, Connector

Book a free consultation with me @ https://calendly.com/coachyesenia/breakthroughdiscoverycall

Author Contact Information

Demetrius N. Booth

Demetrius N. Booth hails from the South Side of Chicago where he was born and raised. He has served in the United States Air Force for twenty-three years and is the founder of **Elevating Purpose Consulting LLC**. He has a dialogical-xenosophia approach to life and religion and strives to be known as a Lighthouse for others navigating the darkness. With teaching as his purpose, he uses his gift to heal the fractured world one person at a time. He has been married to his wife, Marilyn for twenty-four years, and they have gifted the world four beautiful souls: Nia, Imani, Niama, and Demetrius Jr.

In addition to being the Chief Vision Officer and founder of **Elevating Purpose Consulting**, he is a highly rated adjunct instructor with progressive experience in creating positive climates, developing cohesion, focusing purpose, and leading team and organizational learning.

Demetrius has been recognized for his keen ability to yield optimal results in volatile, uncertain, competitive, and ambiguous environments. He has a proven track record of success in curriculum development, seminar and workshop facilitation, keynote speaking, and innovative teaching methodologies for human capital development. Scan this QR Code to go to his Website.

Granny Lisa Kraft

Connect with Granny Lisa Kraft

Come connect with us on our website " Vets Coming Clean".

Vets Coming Clean is a network of like-minded individuals who are providing a voice for Veterans, First-Responders, and anyone who has experiences to share for the rest of us to learn from.

Our podcast uplifts our community through sharing. This helps each of us to find understanding, compassion, and healing.

WWW.VETSCOMINGCLEAN.COM

Mike Montiel

"All Mike" is a proud member of the Pascua Yaqui Tribal Nation and also comes from a long line of blue-collar workers who taught lessons in agriculture, construction, and leadership. 'All Mike's' deep love for his hometown, Superior AZ, is reflected in the local community work he does. He is a founder and currently the vice-president and executive board member for **Rebuild Superior Inc.**, a regional community and economic development organization that positively impacts housing, entrepreneurship, supporting local businesses, as well as arts and culture. He also currently serves as a founder and executive board member for **Regenerating Sonora**, which impacts local food sustainability and works to create a bioregional regenerative process that will impact the entire Sonoran Desert.

Veterans supporting other veterans is one of the most powerful ways that warfighters, like 'All Mike' are able to carry many of the burdens common to military service. Acknowledging and engaging with this has been an obsession of Mike's since he himself experienced an extremely acute bout of PTSD, in which he lost everything and became homeless, after dropping out of college. It is because of the many experiences in the sphere of veterans' service organizations that 'All Mike' has had, that have led him to hold the current titles he has: Commander for **American Legion Post #17** in AZ, Veteran Engagement Specialist on the leadership team for **The Mission Continues Phoenix, Platoon,** AZ state representative for **Mission 22**, and veteran peers support team member with **Operation Shockwave**

Between community activism and support of his military family, 'All Mike' found a love for growing things. He started a business growing mushrooms after he graduated from college, then began a certification program, which gave him a deep understanding of organic farming and ranching. He currently uses this knowledge to support community gardens, farms, and food forests around Arizona.

Currently 'All Mike' provides services to support non-profit organizations, which are seeking guidance in organization, creation, and governance, as well as, facilitated board support, which can focus on specific projects or programs, or focus on overall organizational culture and development. 'All Mike' has been harnessing his story to inspire people for years. He now offers this service to others though he prefers to call it "inspirational oration". He uses his stories to uplift and give hope to others by blending storytelling, humor, and raw emotion. 'All Mike'

Author Contact Information

also provides services in support of farms, ranches, and community agriculture, looking to engage with an experienced individual who has the knowledge, education, passion, and organization to help ensure success on any scale.

If you have a problem, if no one else can help, and you can find him, maybe you can hire, 'All Mike'.

Connect with Mike Montiel:

https://linktr.ee/AllMikeUSA

Ready to Transform

Daniel and Michelle Faust

We at Learn & Live help military/veterans/first responders transform their lives—from the Prayer Room to the Boardroom

We deliver this transformation through speaking, teaching, and content creation.

From our newest book, to attending our Mastermind, to scheduling a 1-on1 thriving session, to following us on social media—all can be found through the QR code below.

Author Contact Information

Scan this code to start your transformation.

Survival is over.

Thriving is your new mission.

Let us empower you for your next mission.

PERFORMANCE & LEADERSHIP
COACHING

Kurt Porter

CORPORATE TRAINING

"I've developed these trainings to both standout and resonate at the same time, to get your team to think differently, while at the same time provide them with immediate skills."
  -Kurt Porter

PUBLIC SPEAKING

COACHING

Author Contact Information

SCHEDULE A CONSULTATION TODAY!

501 S. Moody Ave. Suite 1127
Tampa, Florida, 33609
813-537-3332

kurt.porter@plconfire.com

www.ingramcontent.com/pod-product-compliance
Lightning Source LLC
LaVergne TN
LVHW010338070526
838199LV00065B/5754